Fifty Years of Official Bilingualism

Challenges, Analyses and Testimonies

Invenire Books

INVENIRE is an Ottawa-based "idea factory" specializing in collaborative governance and stewardship. INVENIRE and its authors offer creative and practical responses to the challenges and opportunities faced by today's complex organizations.

INVENIRE welcomes a range of contributions – from conceptual and theoretical reflections, ethnographic and case studies, and proceedings of conferences and symposia, to works of a very practical nature – that deal with problems or issues on the governance and stewardship front. INVENIRE publishes works in French and English.

This is the twenty-fifth volume published by INVENIRE.

INVENIRE also publishes a quarterly electronic journal, found at www.optimumonline.ca.

The titles published by INVENIRE are listed at the end of this book.

Fifty Years of Official Bilingualism

Challenges, Analyses and Testimonies

EDITED BY

Richard Clément
School of Psychology and
Official Languages and Bilingualism Institute
and
Pierre Foucher
Faculty of law
UNIVERSITY of OTTAWA

INVENIRE
Ottawa, Canada
2014

INVENIRE © 2014

Library and Archives Canada Cataloguing in Publication

50 years of official bilingualism : challenges, analyses and testimonies / edited by Richard Clément, School of Psychology and Official Languages and Bilingualism Institute, and Pierre Foucher, Faculty of Law, University of Ottawa.

Issued also in French under title: 50 ans de bilinguisme officiel.
Issued in print and electronic formats.
ISBN 978-1-927465-18-9 (pbk.).--ISBN 978-1-927465-19-6 (html)

1. Canada. Royal Commission on Bilingualism and Biculturalism. 2. Bilingualism--Canada. I. Clément, Richard, 1951-, editor II. Foucher, Pierre, 1956-, editor III. Title: Fifty years of official bilingualism.

FC145.B55F53 2014   306.44'60971   C2014-907002-0
                                                  C2014-907003-9

Invenire and the editors would like to gratefully acknowledge the financial support of the Commissioner of Official Languages of Canada for the publication of this book.

Published by Invenire
P.O. Box 87001
Ottawa, Canada K2P 1X0
www.invenire.ca

Cover design by Sandy Lynch
Back cover photo of the author by Mélanie Cossette
Layout and design by Sandy Lynch

Printed in Canada by Imprimerie Gauvin

Distributed by:
Commoners' Publishing
631 Tubman Cr.
Ottawa, Canada K1V 8L6
Tel.: 613-523-2444
Fax: 888-6134-0329
sales@commonerspublishing.com
www.commonerspublishing.com

RECYCLED
Paper made from
recycled material
FSC
www.fsc.org FSC® C100212

Table of Contents

Testimonies

Profiles of the Authors

List of Authors

Andy Anstett, former Manitoba MLA and Cabinet minister

Maurice Beaudin, Professor of Economics and Geography, Université de Moncton, Shippagan Campus

François Boileau, French Language Services Commissioner of Ontario

Richard Clément, Professor of Psychology and Director, Official Languages and Bilingualism Institute, University of Ottawa

Pierre Curzi, Actor, Political Commentator and President, *Mouvement démocratique pour une constitution du Québec*

Stéphane Dion, member of Parliament, Saint-Laurent – Cartierville

Éric Forgues, Executive Director, Canadian Institute for Research on Linguistic Minorities

Pierre Foucher, Professor of Law, University of Ottawa

Graham Fraser, Commissioner of Official Languages of Canada

Raymond-M. Hébert, Professor Emeritus, Université de Saint-Boniface

Michelle Landry, Professor of Sociology, Université de Moncton, Shippagan Campus

Matthieu LeBlanc, Associate Professor, Department of Translation and Languages, Université de Moncton

Albert Nolette, Associate, Field LLP, Edmonton

Mark Power, Partner, Power Law, Ottawa

Perri Ravon, Lawyer, Power Law, Ottawa

Ingride Roy, Instructor, law faculties of Université de Montréal and Université de Sherbrooke

Sherry Simon, Professor, Département d'études françaises, Concordia University

Keith Spicer, the first Commissioner of Official Languages of Canada

Roger Turenne, Political Analyst

Preface

I have long been inspired by the Royal Commission on Bilingualism and Biculturalism. I read with great interest the diary that André Laurendeau kept while on the Commission and, for the purposes of research for a book, I also read the journal written by his colleague, F.R. Scott. As Guy Laforest has observed, these two men were both *éminences grises*: Laurendeau, the nationalist and humanist editor of the newspaper, *Le Devoir*, and Scott, a socialist lawyer, defender of human rights, poet, constitutional expert and Dean of Law at McGill University.

I often turn to the writings of these two men to find a balance between the needs of a minority community and the principles of equality. I find that the Commission's research, observations and recommendations are still relevant for all those with an interest in language issues.

The Commission's public sessions confirmed that the issues were understood differently in English Canada and French Canada. Indeed, the Preliminary Report from February 1965 stated the following: "... Canada, without being fully conscious of the fact, is passing through the greatest crisis in its history."[1]

Two years later, in the first report, André Laurendeau contributed to what are still called "the famous blue pages," in which he defined terms and concepts relating to a bilingual society. In the same report, the commissioners recommended that Parliament confirm that English and French were the two official languages in Canada and had equal status, that the position of Commissioner of Official Languages be created, and that the person holding that position be a "linguistic ombudsman" and the "active conscience" of linguistic duality.

[1] *Royal Commission on Bilingualism and Biculturalism*, (Ottawa: Queen's Printer, February 1, 1965), p. 5.

The official languages bill was introduced in 1968 and the *Official Languages Act* was enacted in 1969. I am the sixth Commissioner, and I am responsible for ensuring that federal institutions fulfil their duties under the Act.

It was therefore a pleasure for me to participate in a lecture series organized with Canadian universities to commemorate the 50th anniversary of the Commission's creation. I would like to thank Richard Clément from the Official Languages and Bilingualism Institute (OLBI) and Serge Blais from the Centre for Continuing Education of the University of Ottawa for their collaboration and their work. This memorable lecture series has shown the asymmetry of language issues in Canada and the differences among Francophone communities.

At the initial conference, Keith Spicer, the first Commissioner of Official Languages, proved that he had lost none of his spirit or his passion, displaying the energy and keen mind that have been his hallmark since he was Commissioner. These qualities were still in evidence in the lecture given at the University of Ottawa, followed by a conversation we had about his experience as commissioner. I would add that the series created some unforgettable memories.

Also at the University of Ottawa, Ingride Roy analyzed the impact of the Commission's Book IV, *The Cultural Contribution of the Other Ethnic Groups*. She noted that the findings concerning the problems experienced by ethnic groups are still relevant. "While the reality and face of immigration have greatly changed and continue to change the landscape of Canadian society, the problems experienced by ethnic groups remain essentially the same."

At McGill University, Pierre Curzi looked at the audience before starting his speech and said: "But is no one wearing headphones?", thinking that there would be simultaneous interpretation. A voice from the audience answered: "It's because everyone speaks French."

This gives an indication of the changes that have taken place in the Anglophone minority community in Quebec. Fifty years ago when the Commission was created, such an answer would have been unthinkable. Anglophones gathered for a lecture at the McGill Faculty Club would have been overwhelmingly unilingual. Now Quebec's Anglophones are more bilingual than the Francophones.

At the Montreal conference, participants heard two completely contradictory descriptions of the language situation in speeches by Pierre Curzi and Stéphane Dion. Some predicted that the two men would be careful not to be in the same room at the same time, but those in attendance were treated to a very civilized exchange between these two men with very different ideas.

At the same conference, Sherry Simon of Concordia University put official bilingualism in perspective:

Official bilingualism is necessary. Necessary but not sufficient. It is one way in which Canadian reality is expressed, and this way has become essential to the integration of Quebec within the Canadian federation. Federal official bilingualism should be defended not as an expression of a superior humanistic culture or as a form of altruism, but as a strategic recognition of Francophone minorities across the country as well as Quebec national identity into a now fully integrated understanding of citizenship.

Participants at the conference organized at the Université de Saint-Boniface heard from Roger Turenne, who held the first designated bilingual position in Manitoba's public service. He told us about the language debates in the Manitoban context, from Duff Roblin to Premiers Doer and Selinger.

For more than 20 years now, bilingualism in government in Manitoba has been part of a broad consensus both in the political sphere and among what might be called the elites of Manitoba society," he concluded. "It is a consensus that originated with the creation of the B and B Commission half a century earlier.

Raymond-M. Hébert, a veteran of the language debates in Manitoba, talked about successes – such as the Association of Manitoba's Bilingual Municipalities, the Economic Development Council for Manitoba Bilingual Municipalities and the St. Boniface Health Centre – and setbacks, and the risk presented by what he called "a certain sense of lost momentum, if not apathy."

I would like to note that one of the most memorable speeches in the entire series was the one given by Andy Anstett, a former minister in Howard Pawley's government. Despite knowing that he would lose his seat, he agreed to sponsor the bill affirming French as an official language in Manitoba. The government backed down under pressure from the majority. Mr. Anstett, abandoned by his party, did, in fact, lose his seat and left the province. For those attending the lecture, it was a modest account of political courage, and Mr. Anstett was visibly touched by the ovation he received.

At Glendon College in Toronto, several activists from community organizations shared their experiences. François Boileau summarized the progress made by the Franco-Ontarian community and the challenges awaiting it, referring, in particular, to the adoption of the inclusive definition of Francophone.

The Université de Moncton is a renowned language policy research centre, and the conference showed that its reputation is justified. Matthieu LeBlanc shared the results of his research on language of work in the federal public service, which led him to conclude that workplaces are governed by all kinds of power relationships, which are an important factor in language choices. *But overall, the policy's main flaw lies in its implementation, since it is implemented with no regard for the specific nature and needs of the regions and linguistic communities involved,"* he stated. "Because of its internal contradictions, the language policy also contributes to maintaining the domination of English as the language of work and,* ipso facto, *helps maintain certain inequalities between Anglophones and Francophones.*

The implementation of the Act therefore remains incomplete when it comes to the language of work.

Michelle Landry gave a presentation on the legacy of the Laurendeau-Dunton Commission and the principle of cultural equality. Mark Power, Perri Ravon and Albert Nolette looked at Book V of the Report, *The Federal Capital,* and noted that the Ontario government has never taken the interventionist approach recommended by the Commission to create an officially bilingual capital.

This preface provides only a glimpse of the rich contributions made to this series of events, each of which reflected the variety of situations observed across the country. However, two common threads ran through all the presentations. On the one hand, it was clear that Canada has made enormous progress in the area of official languages in the past 50 years. But it was also clear that a great deal of work still needs to be done to achieve the Commission's fundamental goal of equal status for both official languages.

Graham Fraser
Commissioner of Official Languages

Fifty Years Later: The Legacy of the Royal Commission on Bilingualism and Biculturalism[1]

Graham Fraser

I feel particularly privileged to have been able to witness first hand, from the very beginning, the progression of the duality and diversity issue.

I was a university student in the 1960s when André Laurendeau, Davidson Dunton, Frank Scott and the other members of the Royal Commission on Bilingualism and Biculturalism were examining the issue that then divided the country. As a journalist and author, I spent my career studying this particular aspect of Canadian identity. Today, as Commissioner, I continue to follow the issue closely.

It is particularly appropriate to have the event here at Glendon, which was conceived very much in the spirit of the Royal Commission.

And, I confess, it is a bit intimidating to be giving this lecture in the presence of Ken McRoberts, who began his career working for the Royal Commission.

---

[1] Presented on the occasion of the *Forum de la Francophonie Torontoise*, held at Glendon College on March 22, 2013, as part of the celebrations marking the 50th anniversary of the Royal Commission on Bilingualism and Biculturalism.

He was but one of a talented generation of political scientists, historians and sociologists who contributed to the work of the Royal Commission, including such notable York University academics as Ramsay Cook and Irving Abella.

Glendon College is, in fact, an ideal place to be celebrating this anniversary.

The founding principal, Escott Reid, was, in the words of Trent University historian Alyson King, "single-minded and passionate in pursuit of his guiding vision of Glendon as a fully bilingual, fully residential, liberal arts college."[2] And, of course, my predecessor – and Ken McRoberts' predecessor here at Glendon – is Dyane Adam, the distinguished former commissioner of official languages.

First of all, what is a royal commission?

My late brother once had a political science professor at McGill who, in the early 1950s, described it this way: "What is a royal commission? I'll tell you what a Royal Commission is – $100 a day plus expenses!"

More seriously, the late Allan Blakeney described it as "the most traditional form of consultation," adding "Indeed, a case can be made that for at least the last half-century, royal commissions and their reports have been a dominant force in shaping public policy in Canada."[3] Jane Jenson described royal commissions as institutions that represent ideas, that have been "locales for some of the major shifts in the ways that Canadians debate representations of themselves, their present and their futures," adding "They set out the terms of who we are, where we have been and what we might become."[4]

The Royal Commission on Bilingualism and Biculturalism was a special case. Nelson Wiseman has written that "In the 1960s, biculturalism served as a template for the most noteworthy

---

[2] Alyson King. 2004. "The Glendon College Experiment" in Greg Donaghy, Stéphane Roussel, eds. *Escott Reid: Diplomat and Scholar*. Montreal, QC: McGill-Queen's University Press, p. 117.

[3] Allan Blakeney and Sandford Borins. 1998. *Political Management in Canada*. Second Edition. Toronto, ON: University of Toronto Press, p. 187.

[4] Jane Jenson. 1994. "Commissioning Ideas: Representation and Royal Commissions" in Susan D. Phillips, ed. *How Ottawa Spends*. Ottawa, ON: Carleton University Press, p. 39-40.

royal commission of that decade."[5] As Richard Van Loon and Michael Whittington put it in their political science textbook, *The Canadian Political System*, it "featured nine commissioners with a staff of hundreds, and managed, for a few brief years, to eliminate, almost completely, unemployment among Canadian social scientists."[6]

However, even in the early 1970s, there was a dissident academic view. In 1972, Donald Smiley, a political scientist with roots in Western Canada, called the reports of the Royal Commission the leading expression of what he called "the emergent orthodoxy," which meant that residents of Western Canada "have come to feel outside the mainstream of national life by the acceptance in Ottawa ... of Canada and of the Canadian experience which has little relevance to western life and traditions."[7]

Other academics, who have adopted the post-structural framework and vocabulary of hegemony and what one called "the durability of the white-settler bilingual/bicultural formulation in the present, and its contemporary mode of ordering racialized immigrant others," take a more critical view of royal commissions.

Eve Haque argues that the Commission legitimized the dominant role of English and French in Canada and marginalized immigrants and Aboriginal peoples. As she put it, "The establishment of the link between language and race in the crucible of modernity meant that, in contemporary nation-building projects – as that of the B and B Commission – language could become the basis of the Other's exclusion."[8]

---

[5] Nelson Wiseman. 2007. *In Search of Canadian Political Culture*. Vancouver, BC: UBC Press, p. 94.

[6] Richard Van Loon and Michael Whittington. 1987. *The Canadian Political System: Environment, Structure and Process*. Toronto, ON: McGraw-Hill Ryerson Ltd., p. 497.

[7] Donald V. Smiley. 1972. *Canada in Question: Federalism in the Seventies*. Toronto, ON: McGraw-Hill Ryerson Ltd., p. 179, quoted by Kenneth McRoberts. 1989. "Making Canada Bilingual: Illusions and Delusions of Federal Language Policy," in David P. Sugarman and Reg Whitaker, eds. *Federalism and Political Community: Essays in Honour of Donald Smiley*. Peterborough, ON. Broadview Press, p. 141.

[8] Eve Haque. 2012. *Multiculturalism Within a Bilingual Framework: Language, Race, and Belonging in Canada*. Toronto, ON: University of Toronto Press, p. 17.

What I would like to do in this lecture is to describe the social and political context that led to the creation of the Royal Commission, the tensions that marked the Commission's deliberations, and how those tensions have been reflected, half a century later, in the current debate over language policy in Canada.

The idea of a royal commission was first proposed in January 1962 by André Laurendeau in an editorial in *Le Devoir* and, in July 1963, the Royal Commission was announced.

That year and a half was a turbulent time in Quebec. In June 1962, the Conservatives lost their majority and become a minority government, thanks to the election of 26 Social Credit MPs from Quebec. In September, Premier Jean Lesage called an election that was fought over the takeover of Quebec's private hydroelectric companies, winning re-election in November. Throughout the fall, led by House Leader Gilles Grégoire, the *Créditistes* MPs raised the question of French-language services in Parliament and in Ottawa on a daily basis: the Orders of the Day were in English only, the menu of the Parliamentary Restaurant was in English only, the MPs' paycheques were in English only, the security guards were unilingual Anglophones, the announcements at the station were in English only, the service on what was then called Trans-Canada Airlines was in English only ... the list was interminable. Grégoire spoke or asked questions 134 times in the first 60 days. The federal government operated in English.

On November 19, Donald Gordon, the President of Canadian National Railways, appeared before the House of Commons Railway Committee – and Mr. Grégoire was waiting to question him about the fact that none of the 17 vice-presidents at CN were French-Canadian. The ensuing controversy resulted in student demonstrations across Quebec, the largest being led by Bernard Landry, then President of the *Association générale des étudiants de l'Université de Montréal.*

On December 18, 1962, Lester Pearson, then Leader of the Opposition, gave a speech calling for the creation of a royal commission, the speech – he said in his memoirs – of which he was the proudest.

The reaction to his speech in Toronto was revealing. While the *Toronto Star* endorsed the idea, *The Globe and Mail* was much more skeptical. "A wiser course, in our view, would be to let Quebec complete the task it has set itself," the editorialist wrote, adding that the province was in good hands and that reforms were underway.

> *If we have patience, the discovery, already made by its leaders, that English is the language of commerce and is as essential to Quebec as to the rest of us, will spread through the populace. We will find wider areas of agreement. French-speaking Canadians will retain their culture, as the Welsh and the Scots have done.*

In some ways, the *Globe*'s position can be seen as a reflection of English-Canada's attitude towards Quebec. English Canadians tended to see Quebec as a conservative, traditional, church-dominated society that was emerging from decades of backwardness and corruption. As Quebec modernized and matured, it would learn English (in 1961, there were three million unilingual Francophones) and become like Scotland and Wales, which were similarly perceived as English-speaking societies that spoke English with a charming accent, and retained a colourful folklore.

It was a view that dripped with condescension.

In February 1963, the *Front de libération du Québec* was founded. In March, three military barracks in Montreal were bombed. In April – in the second bombing that month – Wilfrid O'Neill, a night watchman, was killed.

Also in April, there was a federal election and Lester Pearson became Prime Minister with a minority government. On election night, crossing paths with Laurendeau, Pearson adviser Maurice Lamontagne said they had to talk.

This was the beginning of an extensive courtship of Laurendeau to become co-chair of the Royal Commission that Pearson had promised in December. Laurendeau's reluctance, which was reinforced by some of the people he consulted, was a reflection of his ambivalence.

Davidson Dunton was Laurendeau's co-chair, a man of grace and moderation who was then President of Carleton University. He played an important role in smoothing the tensions between the

Commission and the government, and in keeping the sometimes spiky personalities of the Commission working together – but I think it is fair to say that the key debates, and the principal tension on the Commission, was between Laurendeau's approach and that of Frank Scott.

Laurendeau's hesitation about accepting the offer had a number of aspects: a reluctance to leave *Le Devoir*, and a hesitation about compromising his nationalist views. But I also think that there was a fundamental question of trust: could he trust the country?

A year before, he had written a best-selling book that was in part a memoir of his own experience 20 years earlier: *La crise de la conscription*. The most well-known quote from his book can be found in the preface: "It is when two nations intensely oppose one another that the extent to which they exist can be measured" [translation]. In his book, Laurendeau explains the theory that the King government had made a pact with French-Canadians: in exchange for participating in the war, there would never be conscription. Thus, to him, the 1942 plebiscite was not a political ruse; it was a betrayal. "In short, French-Canadian nationalists were opposed to the very principle of the plebiscite," [translation] he wrote. They were staunchly against the government asking the majority to erase a promise made to the minority. They rejected the validity of the response from Canadians before it was ever obtained.

"The pact they [French Canadians] were referring to was moral in nature. Parliament could legally impose conscription. What the French-Canadian minority was asking the majority to do was prevent Parliament from doing what it had the political power to do" [translation]. As a result, the internal debate Laurendeau launched in the spring of 1963 was above all a moral debate. And the key question was the existential one that he and Davidson Dunton asked at the beginning of every public hearing: "Can English-speaking and French-speaking Canadians live together, and do they want to? Under what conditions? And are they prepared to accept those conditions?" The questions struck at the core of the existence of the country.

As Commissioner, he was particularly sensitive to the needs of Quebec as a majority French-speaking society, writing in his journal in August 1965: "Bilingualism can only live if it is supported by two unilingualisms, without which bilingualism is a transitory situation which results in the unilingualism of the strongest and most numerous."[9]

F.R. Scott

When he was approached to be on the Commission, Frank Scott was Dean of Law at McGill – 10 years after having been passed over because of his left-wing views. A socialist, one of the authors of the *Regina Manifesto*, a poet, a constitutional lawyer and a strong defender of civil rights, Scott had first got to know Laurendeau during the late 1930s, when both were trying to build bridges between French and English intellectuals in Montreal.

He also had a formative influence on Pierre Elliott Trudeau. As Barry Strayer has written, "Of [Trudeau's] early constitutional mentors who were politically engaged, the most influential was F.R. Scott."[10]

It was as a member of the Royal Commission that F.R. Scott's views on language and bilingualism would be challenged, sharpened and, in some cases, rejected. He had always been clear in his views. As a constitutional lawyer, he took a far-reaching interpretation of section 133 of the *British North America Act*, arguing in 1947 that "British Columbia is already, in an important aspect, a bilingual province."[11]

Scott was named as the only representative of the English minority in Quebec. That role was a key to his identity in many ways: he knew all the Quebec members of the Commission and, with the exception of Dunton, none of the members from the rest of Canada, even though he had a national reputation.

Laurendeau and Dunton were co-chairs, but the real debate, intellectual and emotional, linguistic and national, was between Laurendeau and Scott. Both men had subtle minds, political

[9] Graham Fraser. 2006. *Sorry, I Don't Speak French*. Toronto, ON: McClellend & Stewart Ltd., p. 67.

[10] Barry L. Strayer. 2013. *Canada's Constitutional Revolution*. Edmonton, AB: University of Alberta Press.

[11] F.R. Scott. 1977. "Canada, Quebec, and Bilingualism" in *Essays on the Constitution: Aspects of Canadian Law and Politics*. Toronto, ON: University of Toronto Press, p. 197.

idealism, personal charisma, and poets' sensibilities. As Laforest puts it in his essay on the two men, both were *"éminences grises,"* or intellectual leaders of Quebec and English-speaking Canada, respectively.

Scott's view was that, although French Canada could legitimately be considered a nation, Quebec was – or should be – a bilingual society. His ideal was that the bilingual model should be extended to Canada as a whole, so that the limited rights defined in the *British North America Act* would be extended and the language rights that had been extinguished in Manitoba, Saskatchewan and Alberta would be restored.

It took Scott some time to come to terms with Laurendeau's view of the need for two unilingualisms – a view that had been adopted by one of the researchers, William Mackey.

> *In regard to this idea of promoting unilingualism, I confess that, perhaps lacking French logic, I could not see how a Commission appointed to promote bilingualism could end up by favouring the promotion of unilingualism,"* Scott wrote in his journal. *"Gradually it dawned on me, and I think on the others, that what Mackey meant was that unless there was a strong degree of unilingualism in the bilingual country for each language, one would eventually dominate and assimilate the other.*[12]

Laurendeau's view, eloquently expressed in the blue pages of the first volume of the Royal Commission's report, was that the survival of French in Canada and North America depended upon a strong, French-speaking society in Quebec and, as he wrote in his journal, two unilingualisms.

While Scott admired Laurendeau's independence of thought and opposition to Duplessis, he occasionally fulminated at the myths he felt that Laurendeau perpetuated about the English community: "Only in the economic area do the English have a privileged place. In ... other activities, as well as in politics, it is a handicap to belong to the English minority."[13]

But both men were appalled by the ignorance and prejudice they encountered toward French in Canada during the Commission's visits to Western Canada. Both were also taken

---

[12] Graham Fraser. 2006. *op. cit.,* p. 66.
[13] *Ibid.,* p. 62.

aback by the degree to which separatists were dominating public discussion in Quebec.

Scott did not lose his quick wit during some of those stormy hearings. At a meeting in Sherbrooke, a young man said that he cared nothing about the French-speaking minorities outside Quebec, that the only minority that mattered was the English-speaking minority in Quebec, and it should leave as soon as possible. *"J'y suis, j'y reste"* (I'm here, I'm staying), responded Scott.

In the discussions in the fall of 1967, he found himself in a minority: as he put it, "the only voice for a bilingual Quebec." He ultimately dissented from the Commission's recommendations in Volume 4, arguing that, by recommending the working language in Quebec be French, it was contradicting its earlier rejection of a territorial solution to the language issue.

The final note that Scott struck was a pessimistic one: a 10-page, legal-sized document, poignantly titled "The End of the Affair." It is undated, but on the basis of the internal evidence it was written in 1970, before the October Crisis. Though the Commission's work was over, Scott wrote, the crisis in Quebec was not – and he warned that the recommendations could not solve all the problems of national unity. He closed "on a personal note":

> It is astonishing and also frightening for me to watch Quebec abandon so many of its ancient virtues and values in order to rush into the North American capitalist system with arms open for the embrace. The values of that system I learned to despise and reject in the 1930s. I had hoped that the Catholic tradition with its greater emphasis on social obligations would somehow mitigate the prevailing Protestant ethic of free enterprise.

It is a poignant sign of age that at 70 he nostalgically saw "virtues and values," whereas at 33 he had denounced the Church for interpreting the Depression "as a sort of punishment from God upon greedy individuals."[14]

The public sessions of the Royal Commission confirmed some of the conceptual problems in its mandate.

---

[14] *Ibid.*, p. 76-77.

But what emerged as the essential debate, and the source of critical tension within the Royal Commission, was the conceptual model that should be developed for Canada. André Laurendeau felt that the central problem was Quebec's fragility as a French-speaking society, and that this should be the primary consideration. Frank Scott, on the other hand, felt that Quebec was, legally, constitutionally and practically, a bilingual province – and that bilingual status should be extended to the rest of Canada. Both agreed that the status quo – which Pearson had described in his December 1962 speech as "an English-speaking Canada with a bilingual Quebec" – was unacceptable. But their ultimate visions of what the future should be were quite different.

Paradoxically, both felt that they had lost. When Volume 1 was published, Laurendeau said bleakly to a colleague: "It does nothing for Quebec." For Scott, on the contrary, Laurendeau had been pushing for a constitutional change to give more powers to Quebec, which Scott thought to be completely inappropriate, and he felt that the commissioners and their researchers were much too sympathetic to the idea of a unilingual French-speaking Quebec. Scott would ultimately dissent from the Commission's recommendation that the language of work in Quebec be French, arguing that this was inconsistent with the earlier rejection of territorial bilingualism. "This is exactly what I knew would happen," he wrote grimly in his journal.[15]

The legacy of the Royal Commission

It is easy to forget how controversial the Royal Commission was, and how much it was criticized: first, for its Preliminary Report, which stated that Canada was passing through the greatest crisis in its history – a crisis that few English-speaking Canadians recognized or acknowledged – and then at the expense and length of time the Commission took.

It is also easy to forget how difficult it was for the commissioners to reach a consensus. In March 1968, Laurendeau brought Scott and Paul Lacoste together to hammer out a

[15] *Ibid.*, p. 75.

constitutional point. They finally reached an agreement – on the fourteenth draft.[16]

In retrospect, the controversies vanished, and the conflicts were smoothed over. What remains are the observations, the recommendations and the studies.

The observations were clear sighted. I quote: "Anyone who speaks French still runs the risk of this kind of insult: 'Speak white;' 'Why don't you speak a white man's language?' (an insult that manages, in retrospect, to be simultaneously racist and sexist); 'If you want to speak French, go back to your province;' or simply 'Why don't you speak English?'"[17]

That discourse of discrimination and insult has virtually disappeared in Canada – in part because it was so clearly flushed out into the open by the Royal Commission. The description of Canada going through a crisis was derided in 1965; in 1967, after the defeat of the Liberals in Quebec and General de Gaulle's *"Vive le Québec libre,"* there was a general recognition that the commissioners had a point.

The famous *"page bleues,"* which Laurendeau wrote, coined the phrase that Quebec was a "distinct society" and – while purporting to be simply a glossary of terms – sketched, with great sensitivity, the realities of language contact, language dominance, the role of Quebec in promoting and protecting the French fact in Canada, and the realities facing linguistic minorities.

Let me quote just one example:

> *We shall mention later the difficulties, which may be dramatic in their intensity, faced by a bilingual person who must work in his second language—his sense of being diminished, the irritation which frequently results, and his loss of efficiency,"* Laurendeau wrote. *"There are situations in which this choice is unavoidable, especially when an individual is almost the only speaker of his language in a given environment. But the objective should be to impose*

---

[16] André Laurendeau. 1990. *Journal tenu pendant la Commission royale d'enquête sur le bilinguisme et le biculturalisme.* Outremont, QC : VLB/Septentrion, p. 43.

[17] Government of Canada. 1965. *A Preliminary Report of the Royal Commission on Bilingualism and Biculturalism,* p. 86, paragraph 80.

the fewest possible sacrifices from which nobody benefits—
neither the individual, nor his employers.[18]

And the recommendations?

Some are now taken for granted: that English and French be formally declared the official languages of Canada, that there be an official languages act, and that there be a commissioner of official languages. Others have proven less durable: the designation of bilingual districts, and that New Brunswick, Quebec and Ontario become officially bilingual.

But there are less obvious, even more important legacies that the Royal Commission has left us.

An official languages policy as well as a multiculturalism policy flowed from its recommendations, as it laid the framework not only for linguistic duality but also for cultural diversity as Canadian values.

It established a framework of language rights that shaped both the *Official Languages Act* and the Canadian Charter of Rights and Freedoms, establishing as quasi-constitutional Canada's language regime. This, in turn, led to the creation of French-language schools and school boards across Canada – and the right to a trial in the official language of choice of the accused.

This has meant that, in Toronto, there is French-language television and radio, including provincial educational television, and a French-language theatre company. There are also 24 French-language primary and secondary schools,[19] and health services in French.

And in Ontario, we have bilingual drivers' licences and health cards, a *French Language Services Act*, an Office of Francophone Affairs with a minister and a deputy-minister, a Commissioner of French-language Services and, as has been the case for many years, a bilingual premier.

For years, sovereignists in Quebec have said that they want Quebec to be as French as Ontario is English. It is not surprising that they do not say that anymore.

---

[18] Government of Canada. 1967. *Report of the Royal Commission on Bilingualism and Biculturalism*, Volume 1, paragraph 32.

[19] http://www.familycare.utoronto.ca/camps_schools/french_schools.html.

For the country, the result has been, in effect, a compromise between the beliefs, goals and convictions of both André Laurendeau and Frank Scott.

That compromise, that wrestling between individual rights and collective rights, can be seen in the work of Canadian philosopher Charles Taylor, in his essay "The Politics of Recognition,"[20] and of Will Kymlicka, in *Politics in the Vernacular: Nationalism, Multiculturalism, and Citizenship.*[21] Both accept what Taylor calls "a politics of difference,"[22] and Kymlicka calls "a post-ethnic conception of minority nationalism:"[23] a compromise between collective rights and individual rights that protects the idea of cultural survival.

That sense of compromise between individual and collective rights is now part of the Canadian political and judicial landscape – on the one hand, a clear recognition of French predominance in Quebec, where French is the language of work and the language of public interaction and – at the same time, a federal recognition of language rights as human rights that are guaranteed in a Charter and respected across the country.

It is a legacy to be proud of.

[20] Published in Charles Taylor and Amy Gutmann. 1992. *Multiculturalism and "The Politics of Recognition": An Essay.* Princeton, NJ: Princeton University Press.

[21] Will Kymlicka. 2001. *Politics in the Vernacular: Nationalism, Multiculturalism, and Citizenship.* Oxford, UK: Oxford University Press.

[22] *Ibid.*, p. 61.

[23] *Ibid.*, p. 287.

2

French, the Common Language of Quebec[1]

Pierre Curzi

I would like to start by thanking Will Straw and the McGill Institute for the Study of Canada for taking the risk of inviting this "hawk", as Don Macpherson describes me. In fact, I am neither as dangerous nor as fearsome as some might think. I am delighted to have the opportunity to speak today to you Anglophones living in Quebec, since such opportunities are very rare.

Let us begin with the Laurendeau-Dunton Commission: in the 1960s, that Commission confirmed the existence of bilingualism and biculturalism in Canada, which, in my opinion, are two utopian ideas whose adverse effects are multiplying. This being said, the Laurendeau-Dunton Commission did have some positive outcomes: first and foremost, it gave Canada's French minorities, who were often particularly mistreated in their respective provinces, both rights and institutions.

The second positive outcome of the Commission was that it established real bilingualism in the federal public service and thereby contributed to the bilingualism of many Anglo-Canadians and Franco-Quebecers. Thanks to the Commission, many people have been able to learn, function, work and provide services at

[1] Paper presented during the "Does Bilingualism Have a Future in Canada?" conference held at McGill University on May 1, 2013, as part of the celebrations marking the 50th anniversary of the Royal Commission on Bilingualism and Biculturalism.

the federal level in both languages. I want to emphasize a major distinction that is often overlooked, namely that individual bilingualism, trilingualism and multilingualism are undeniable personal assets. What I adamantly oppose is the institutional bilingualism imposed on Quebec.

I will take this opportunity to tell you a short personal anecdote. In 1968 and 1969, I was part of the *Théâtre du Nouveau Monde* young actors' tour, which gave us a chance to perform in French in front of all the Francophone communities across Canada. I was about 20 years old at the time, and I came to two main realizations. First, most people in Canada function in English. Next, small Francophone groups in Canada are especially at risk, which is understandable given that they are a very small minority within a very large majority. There is, therefore, a fundamental difference between living in French in Quebec and living in French elsewhere in Canada.

I will not dwell on biculturalism, since over time it quickly turned into multiculturalism, a grand illusion that has nothing to do with the true meaning of cultural diversity. In Quebec, this multiculturalism later took on shades of interculturalism as proposed by the Bouchard-Taylor Commission, but I do not want to focus on this question. Regardless of the models proposed, I do not see them as realities. Biculturalism does not exist. There are two major cultures in Canada: a Francophone culture originating mainly in Quebec and an Anglophone culture that tries its best to distinguish itself from its all-powerful American counterpart. In themselves, they are merely two cultural solitudes.

At this point, it is important to provide a little historical background so we can understand our current situation better. Several events took place in Quebec during the time of the Laurendeau-Dunton Commission: the creation and coming into power of the *Parti Québécois*; the Charter of the French language (*Bill 101*); the various incarnations of the *Office québécois de la langue française*; the creation of the *Caisse de dépôt et placement du Québec*; major education and health reforms; large projects and the takeover of hydroelectricity by the Quebec government; the Peace of the Braves; the emergence of a Francophone business class known as "Quebec Inc."; cultural explosion and growth in music, song, theatre, cinema, dance and circus arts; and, finally, the first referendum in 1980, which, in a sense, ended that period. That whole era was experienced by my generation, the baby boomers, as a fight for "national liberation." We liberated ourselves from the domination of a minority that came from a colonizing power; we liberated ourselves from an Anglo-Canadian minority that owned us.

That "national liberation" had many consequences: the end of religious domination; the start of major social reforms in Quebec; and the emergence and strengthening of the Quebec union movement, which finally moved away from its American big brothers. At that time, Quebecers defined themselves as a nation and claimed their place as one of the two founding peoples of Confederation.

That period also had consequences for Quebec Anglophones. First, more than 200,000 Anglo-Canadians left Quebec over 20 years. This was a major loss for the city of Montreal and for Quebec in terms of knowledge, culture, wealth and energy. Indeed, Montreal is still struggling to recover from this terrible loss. This gave rise to the infamous repatriation of the Constitution by the Trudeau government in 1982, with the result that Quebec's political power began to weaken, later leading us to the *Clarity Act*.

What was happening on the language front during that time? Many have talked about, and still talk about, a "period of linguistic peace" that is now "threatened" by *Bill 114*. Yet this assertion is totally false. There was no linguistic peace, but instead two hundred attacks against the sections of *Bill 101*, numerous judgments by the Supreme Court of Canada against *Bill 101*, and the Canadian Charter of Rights and Freedoms, which gutted the Charter of the French language and, among other things, imposed the Canada clause rather than the Quebec clause. If we had gotten the Quebec clause, we would not have the problems we are wrestling with now.

Moreover, the Canadian Charter, as a political strategy, granted judges the unbelievable power to give individual rights precedence over collective rights and thus embodied the abdication of political power. What this means is that the unceasing battle against a law that is fundamental to Francophone and Quebec identity should be called "institutional guerrilla warfare" rather than "linguistic peace."

However, I should note the main positive aspect of that turbulent period: Anglo-Canadians became Anglo-Quebecers for real, and not just as a matter of semantics. Anglophones in Quebec became bilingual because they recognized that they were living in Quebec with a Francophone majority. In the same way, Quebec Francophones also became bilingual because they themselves realized that their province was part of an essentially Anglophone country. This aspect was therefore extremely positive, since it enriched us through individual bilingualism, as can be seen in the youth of Montreal today.

Does this make Anglo-Quebecers a minority? Not at all, in my view. I believe that the Francophones of Canada are the only minority, wherever they may live in the country. Anglo-Quebecers are simply an extension of the Anglophone majority in Canada as a whole. Of course, we are carefully leaving out all the Aboriginal nations here. For them, both Anglophones and Francophones have been ruthless exterminators or at least culpable colonizing powers.

To my knowledge, Anglo-Quebecers, as an extension of the Anglophone Canadian majority, have unquestionable economic power, especially in Montreal. Above all, they have political power that is disproportionate to their numbers. It is a complex and disquieting power, since it shackles and fetters the electoral process. Through their monolithic mass vote in favour of the Quebec Liberal Party, supported by certain Francophones and a large number of Allophones, they ensure support for that party and give it an importance that distorts the normal expression of various political currents, which ordinarily encompass the left, the right, the centre and their assorted variations. This polarization toward the Quebec Liberal Party makes it difficult for us to imagine how to avoid a minority government, as is currently the case for the *Parti Québécois*. Not to mention the fact that the Anglophone community, despite its small size (about 10 percent of the population), has a number of ridings in which the elected members usually become ministers later and therefore have significant power in provincial politics.

Anglo-Quebecers are therefore not a minority. Despite making up a small percentage of the Quebec population, the Anglophone community is maintaining its numbers (births and deaths, very few departures from Quebec), and its language vitality index[2] is well above that of Francophones. In 2006, for example, the vitality index was 143 for Anglophones and 109 for Francophones on the island of Montreal, and 130 for Anglophones and 103 for Francophones provincially. This means that Anglophones in Quebec are "attracting" more people than Francophones. It must be said that Anglo-Quebecers can draw on a tremendous and appealing English cultural power, a centre of creation and culture encompassing scientific research, innovation, literature, music and images in all their forms, which no doubt helps them maintain their power and their vitality index.

In short, everything is in English these days. The free market and trade liberalization, unlimited access to means of communication and individual mobility have made the planet a global village as predicted, and the village is currently English-speaking. If we give free rein to natural forces, which are based on the logic of numbers, then we can assume without a shadow of a doubt that bilingualism and institutional bilingualism will soon be implemented throughout Quebec. If Anglo-Quebecers do not voluntarily decide to make French the common language in the workplace, in trade, on signs, in culture, in health, in education and in municipal, provincial and federal governments, and if they do not work toward this vigorously, then Francophones will inevitably be assimilated. And with the assimilation of Francophones, Canada will have lost all real cultural diversity, which, in itself, creates a balance of power that I view as necessary to Canadian democratic life. We will have lost that which we, you and I, value most in the world, namely this difference that uniquely enriches us.

[2] The language vitality index is calculated by dividing the number of speakers of the language as a home language by the number of mother-tongue speakers. See P. Curzi. 2010. *Le grand Montréal s'anglicise: esquisse du vrai visage du français, p. 26, Table 9.* Taken from http://www.pierrecurzi.org/le-grand-montreal-sanglicise/.

3

Does Bilingualism Have a Future in Canada?[1]

Stéphane Dion

Does bilingualism have a future in Canada? Of course it does! Whether it will be optimal or fragmented remains to be seen. Are we going to make substantial improvements in our ability to speak our two official languages, or are we going to be satisfied with doing the minimum?

English-French bilingualism will remain a fundamental characteristic of Canada

Whatever happens, English and French will remain the two languages of choice in Canada. They are part and parcel of our past, and they will shape our future.

The fact that one of these languages is English presents two challenges for us; but in another way, it makes things easier. The first challenge is the power of assimilation that English exercises over Canadian Francophones in a continent that is predominantly English-speaking. The second challenge is that it is difficult to motivate an Anglophone population to learn another language in a world where English is the ideal *lingua franca*.

---

[1] Conference delivered on May 1, 2013 at McGill University at a public event commemorating the 50th anniversary of the launch of the Royal Commission on Bilingualism and Biculturalism entitled "Does bilingualism have a future in Canada?"

However, having English as one of our official languages also gives us a huge advantage: we are in no danger of seeing some other, non-official language asserting itself as the language of communication between our two linguistic communities. In Switzerland, German- and French-speaking young people are using English increasingly to communicate with each other.

French, as an official language of Canada but also an international language, is a logical choice as a second language for English-speaking Canadians. French has more appeal for them than another, less widely used official language would – such as Flemish in Belgium.

Moreover, French is not too difficult for an Anglophone to learn. You really have to get up early to learn Mandarin as a second language!

The fact is that no language threatens the status of French as the second, most widely spoken language in Canada after English. Admittedly, our country is increasingly multicultural, and therefore multilingual, but the Allophone group is very heterogeneous, with over two hundred mother tongues. According to the 2011 Census, English is the mother tongue of 57.8 percent of Canadians and French is the mother tongue of 21.7 percent. In a distant third place is Punjabi, the mother tongue of just 1.4 percent of Canada's population.[2]

It is true that Spanish has gained ground since the signing of NAFTA but not to the point that it threatens the status of French as Canada's second best known language. According to the 2011 census, 2.7 percent of Canadians know Spanish and 30.1 percent, French. Outside of Quebec, 2.1 percent know Spanish and 10.2 percent, French.[3]

One crucial challenge will be to help the 235,000 or so immigrants[4] who come to Canada every year to learn both official languages. A great many of them wish to do so.

---

[2] Government of Canada. 2014. *Census 2011,* "Linguistic Characteristics of Canadians". Ottawa, ON: Statistics Canada. https://www12.statcan.gc.ca/census-recensement/2011/as-sa/98-314-x/98-314-x2011001-eng.cfm.
[3] *Ibid.*
[4] *Ibid.*

Newcomers to Canada show a strong interest in learning both official languages. According to the Canadian Association of Immersion Teachers, children of immigrants do very well in French immersion programs and often achieve better results than Canadian-born Anglophones. According to a study by Canadian Parents for French, the majority of Allophone parents believe that learning both of Canada's official languages would be an asset for their children. There is no evidence that Canada's growing multicultural heterogeneity threatens official bilingualism. On the contrary, there is every indication that the two main components of our diversity can coexist quite happily, and can even merge with one another.

Canada's two official languages will therefore continue to reflect the country's reality, but how many of us will be speaking both of them? Canada is and will remain a country with two official languages, agreed; but to what extent will its population be bilingual?

The progress of bilingualism in Canada

According to the 2011 Census, the proportion of Canadians able to conduct a conversation in both official languages is 17.5 percent. The most bilingual Canadians are Francophones outside Quebec (83.6 percent), followed by Anglophones in Quebec (68.9 percent), Allophones in Quebec (50.2 percent), Francophones in Quebec (35.8 percent), Anglophones outside Quebec (7.4 percent) and Allophones outside Quebec (5.6 percent).[5]

Is bilingualism making progress in Canada? In 1971, 13.5 percent of Canadians spoke both English and French. In 1996, the rate of bilingualism reached 17 percent.[6] Since then, it has been marking time.

---

[5] Government of Canada. 2011. *Census of Population 2011*, "Linguistic Characteristics of Canadians, Language." Ottawa, ON: Statistics Canada, Figure 3. Jean-Pierre Corbeil. 2012. *Immigration, Diversity and Linguistic Duality in Canada: a Brief Overview*. Ottawa, ON: Statistics Canada, September 13.

[6] Government of Canada. 2014. *Census 2011*, "Linguistic Characteristics of Canadians". Ottawa, ON: Statistics Canada. https://www12.statcan.gc.ca/census-recensement/2011/as-sa/98-314-x/98-314-x2011001-eng.cfm.

True, we have made remarkable progress over the last 50 years. Looking at the last decade only, however, we see that in some respects we are no longer making progress. We have to realize this, admit it and summon up fresh energy.

In Quebec, the greatest progress over the last 50 years has been the massive surge in French learning by non-Francophones. In 1963, who would have imagined that in 2013, Quebec's Anglophones would be the most bilingual population in Canada – second only to out-of-Quebec Francophones? That almost 95 percent of Anglophone Quebeckers aged 21 or younger would be bilingual? That the massive linguistic transfers of immigrants towards English, so prevalent in Quebec in 1963, would be more oriented toward French in 2013?

In 1963, and even up to 1990, the Francophone minorities outside Quebec (except in New Brunswick and a few schools in Ontario) did not manage their own education systems. Nowadays, there are Francophone school management structures in all the provinces and territories, and these structures are linked to a network of Francophone high schools, colleges and universities. Nothing like this could have been hoped for in 1963.

Who could have predicted the extraordinary enthusiasm for French immersion schools in provinces with an English-speaking majority? According to the 2011 Census, such schools have an enrolment of at least 329,000![7]

Progress of this kind does not just happen. We had to make choices together, some of them difficult and many perceived as contradictory.

Sure, the *Official Languages Act* and *Bill 101*,[8] or the Charter of Rights and Freedoms[9] and the *Charter of the French Language*[10] might well have different sources of inspiration; but these measures – notwithstanding what their respective supporters might think – do complement one another. They have helped us make linguistic progress on every front.

---

[7] *Ibid.*

[8] *Official Languages Act*, R.S.C., 1985, c. 0-1.

[9] Quebec Charter of the Human Rights and Freedoms, R.S.Q., 1977, c. C-10.

[10] Charter of the French Language, R.S.Q., 1977, c. C-11.

Progress has levelled off in recent years

To gain a better idea of the challenges ahead of us, however, let us take stock of the last few years. According to the most recent Census, the proportion of Canadians able to conduct a conversation in both official languages barely changed between 2006 and 2011: from 17.4 percent of the population to 17.5 percent.[11]

In terms of knowledge of French, we have also levelled off: in 2006, 30.7 percent of Canada's population could conduct a conversation in French, as compared with 30.1 percent in 2011.

In Quebec, the rate of English-French bilingualism rose from 40.6 percent in 2006 to 42.6 percent in 2011. Elsewhere in Canada, it fell from 10.8 percent in 2006 to 10.2 percent in 2011.

The most worrying drop was among young Anglophones living outside Quebec:

> *The proportion of these youth able to conduct a conversation in both of the country's official languages was 15.2% in 1996. It has decreased steadily since then to 11.2% in 2011, a decline of 4 percentage points. Despite a rise in [...] immersion program registrations, the proportion of young people outside Quebec exposed to the instruction of French as a second language over the past 20 years has decreased from 53.3% to 44%.*[12]

This means that outside Quebec, where enrolment in French immersion schools rose by 23 percent between 1991 and 2011, the increase was more than offset by a 23 percent drop in enrolment in regular French-as-a-second-language programs.

This net decrease may be the downside of the popularity of immersion schools. Parents and students with the strongest motivation to learn French rush to them, so that there is less pressure to maintain the learning of French in other schools. Solving this problem is a priority. The Council of Ministers of Education will have to find solutions, and indicate how the federal government can help.

[11] Jean-Pierre Corbeil, *2011 Census of Population. Linguistic Characteristics of Canadians: Canada's Linguistic Duality and Diversity*, Appearance before the House of Commons Standing Committee on Official Languages, November 20, 2012.

[12] *Ibid.*

In this regard, it would be advisable to consult the French-speaking communities outside Quebec, who make up 4.3 percent of the population outside Quebec.[13] Their advice would be invaluable, because they have direct experience of the bilingualization of Anglophones. For them, expansion of the French-language space is a result of the integration of numerous Anglophones into their communities.

Indeed, many young Francophones are forming exogamous couples with Anglophones, getting married and starting families. At least two-thirds of Francophone children outside Quebec are growing up in families in which one of the parents does not have French as their mother tongue. This is the main challenge facing the future of the French language and communities in Canada. Outside Quebec, the transmission of French to the children reaches a rate of 95 percent when both parents are Francophone, but only 42 percent when only one parent speaks French. However, the rate goes up to 70 percent when the non-Francophone parent also speaks French.

Bilingualism in Quebec today

I would say that in Quebec, we still have to convince ourselves that we have nothing to fear from bilingualism. To those who claim that it constitutes a serious threat to French, I would answer: Of course we have to stay vigilant, but there is every indication that the French fact is doing well in Quebec: bilingualism poses no threat to the language of Gilles Vigneault!

According to the most recent census,[14] 94.4 percent of Quebeckers can speak French, 87 percent of them speak it most often (82.5 percent) or regularly (4.5 percent) at home, 89 percent speak it most of the time at work (according to the *Office de la langue française*), and these percentages have changed very little in recent years. In 1951, Quebeckers whose mother tongue was

---

[13] Based on the language spoken most often or regularly at home, a value that remained stable by comparison with the *2006 Census*: Government of Canada. "French and the francophonie in Canada." *Language, 2011 Census of Population.* Ottawa, ON: Statistics Canada.

[14] Government of Canada. "French and the francophonie in Canada," *Language, 2011 Census of Population.* Ottawa, ON: Statistics Canada.

English constituted 14 percent of the population; the figure today is 8 percent. In 2001, language transfers by Allophones were 34.7 percent towards French and 34.0 percent towards English; today, the figures are 40.0 percent towards French and 29.9 percent towards English.

Among the newcomers who settle in Quebec, French is the most known language at time of arrival: 57.9 percent speak French, 50.9 percent English and 24.9 percent neither English nor French.[15]

Admittedly, the percentage of residents who speak only French at home is decreasing in Greater Montreal: in 2001, it was 62.4 percent; in 2006, 59.8 percent; and in 2011, 56.5 percent. There is an explanation for these figures, however. More and more Montreal families speak French and another language: 13.0 percent in 2001; 15.6 percent in 2006; and 18.2 percent in 2011.[16] Montreal, as a great metropolis, experiences growing cultural diversity, intermingling populations and exogamy. It is not that Francophones are abandoning French, but they are falling in love with non-Francophones! No harm in that, right? On the contrary!

In Quebec, *Bill 101* provides very strong protection for the French language; this eliminates the need for any measure designed to restrict the use of English unduly. There is no need to eliminate the bilingual status of municipalities where the proportion of Anglophones has fallen below 50 percent; nor to prevent young Francophones from attending an English-language *cégep* even when they have the necessary grades. Far from serving the cause of French, punitive and fear-driven measures like this can only harm the cause of bilingualism in Quebec.

Bill 101 is far from weakened by the Supreme Court. On the contrary, I would say that Supreme Court decisions have made it more realistic and more acceptable, even to Francophones. No survey indicates that a majority of Quebeckers are or were in favour of unilingual signage. It is reasonable and sensible for

[15] Jean-Pierre Corbeil. 2012. *Immigration, Diversity and Linguistic Duality in Canada: a Brief Overview*. Ottawa, ON: Statistics Canada, September 13.

[16] Government of Canada. "Linguistic Characteristics of Canadians," *Language, 2011 Census of Population*. Ottawa, ON: Statistics Canada, Table 7.

French to be mandatory, and even dominant, in order to better protect French in the North American context. But what is the point of banning other languages? Like the Supreme Court, Quebeckers are against such an attitude.

Consider the recent Quebec "bridge schools" controversy. The Supreme Court ruling did nothing to allow such schools.[17] The Court simply asked the Quebec government to treat each and every case on its own merits in order to avert unfair situations. In response, the Quebec government enacted legislation that limited, to a few per year, the number of students who can take that route to access the Anglophone school system.[18]

Conclusion

As we can see, we can do more and do better to promote the learning of our two official languages. We must do a better job of exploiting the advantages we gain from the international reach of our two official languages. They open many doors and windows on the world for us, leading to a many-faceted cultural, scientific and economic universe in which we obviously have everything to gain by becoming full participants.

Bilingualism is one of our best assets. Canada is one of the few countries whose people can use two official languages of international stature in their everyday lives. We should love them, learn them and use them, in order to derive the greatest possible benefit from them.

---

[17] *N'Guyen v Attorney General of Quebec* [2009] 3 R.S.C. 208.
[18] *An Act to amend the Charter of the French Language*, L.Q. 2010. chapter 23.

4

50 Years After the Laurendeau-Dunton Commission: The Journey of French Ontario[1]

François Boileau

I n 1963, the federal government set up the Royal Commission on Bilingualism and Biculturalism, commonly known as the Laurendeau-Dunton Commission. Following several years of debate and consultation organized across the country, the Commission published a six-volume final report containing countless recommendations. However, the most vocal recommendation remains that French and English be declared official languages not only at the federal level but also in the provinces of Ontario and New Brunswick.

Ontario: a quasiofficial French Language Services Act

In 1969, the federal government responded favourably to the symbolic recommendations made by the Laurendeau-Dunton Commission by enacting the *Official Languages Act*. That Act had an undeniable, though not immediate, impact on the rights of Francophones, particularly in Ontario.

---

[1] Paper presented at Glendon College in Toronto on March 22, 2013 as part of the celebrations marking the 50th anniversary of the Royal Commission on Bilingualism and Biculturalism.

Gentle reforms, guided by a step-by-step approach, were undertaken in Ontario under the Robarts and Davis governments, reforms that culminated in the unanimous passage of the *French Language Services Act* (*FLSA*) by the members of the Legislative Assembly of Ontario in 1986, following some intense backroom negotiations and deals.

The *FLSA* confirms that statutes must be enacted by the Legislative Assembly in both languages at the same time and that every citizen can appear before a court in French or English under the *Courts of Justice Act*. That Act, which gives French and English official language status in Ontario's justice system, was even enacted two years before the *FLSA*.

The *FLSA* is also quasi-constitutional, as the Ontario Court of Appeal confirmed in the Montfort case. In short, not much is needed for the *FLSA* to be an official languages act, just … *the word "official"*, especially in the title!

Though unable to live in an officially bilingual province, Franco-Ontarians have made a number of gains that supplement the *FLSA* and contribute to their vitality.

Gains won and granted

The gains made by Franco-Ontarians in terms of language rights have often been won following battles with public authorities. The best known example remains *Regulation 17*. The schools crisis in Sturgeon Falls in 1971 or in Penetanguishene in 1976 should also be mentioned. More recently, the saga of the Montfort Hospital[2] has shown what a strong Franco-Ontarian community that stands tall can achieve when faced with something unacceptable.

However, many positive measures and initiatives supporting the development and vitality of the Francophone community have been undertaken over the past few decades by the Ontario government when it was not dealing with a language crisis, including the *Aménagement Linguistique Policy* (ALP).

The ALP, which was the first of its kind in the country, was adopted by the Ontario Ministry of Education in 2004 and aims

---

[2] See *Lalonde v. Ontario (Health Services Restructuring Commission)* (2001), 56 O.R. (3d) 505.

to help Ontario's Francophone students preserve their culture, boost their pride and improve their academic performance by addressing their specific needs. Seven years later, the *French Language Policy Framework for Postsecondary Education and Training* was adopted to give Ontario students more opportunities to study and train in French.

Another example is the creation of the Office of the French Language Services Commissioner, the second such provincial office after New Brunswick's. In 2007, the Legislative Assembly amended the *FLSA* to include an independent ombudsman to help the government improve compliance with the letter and spirit of the *FLSA*. Despite this progress, the Francophone community faces many challenges, including those in post-secondary education.

Need for an educational continuum

Since 1982, section 23 of the Canadian Charter of Rights and Freedoms has recognized the right of members of official language minorities to have their children educated in their mother tongue where numbers so warrant. However, it was not until 1998 that Francophones were finally able to manage their own schools in Ontario.

In a minority setting, French-language education protects and passes along the French language and culture needed to ensure the survival of the Franco-Ontarian community. Colleges and universities are an integral part of the educational continuum. They play an important role in the development of the community by training future French-speaking leaders, qualified staff and entrepreneurs, and investors who help make the economy competitive. They also encourage elementary and high school students and their parents to commit to an education in French from the start.

However, Franco-Ontarians, who number more than 600,000,[3] currently have access to only 36 percent of post-secondary education programs in eastern Ontario (compared with those offered in English), 33 percent in northern Ontario and 0 to 3

[3] For more details, see http://www.ofa.gov.on.ca/en/franco-census-2011.html (page consulted in August 2013).

percent in central-southwestern Ontario.[4] These facts speak for themselves.

There is therefore an obvious need for at least more post-secondary programs in French or even, in the long term, for a Franco-Ontarian university. Of course, this takes nothing away from the solid reputation of excellence enjoyed by bilingual universities like Laurentian University and the University of Ottawa.

Depriving Francophone and Francophile students of such options has an impact on Ontario society by making it increasingly incapable of providing equivalent services in French because of a lack of bilingual and French speaking professionals. These students could begin to see French-language studies in elementary and high school as a pointless exercise. And these students are increasingly heterogeneous, just like the Francophone population.

A hybrid, multicultural Francophone community

The Laurendeau-Dunton Commission devoted an entire volume to *The Cultural Contribution of the Other Ethnic Groups*.[5] Acting on the Commission's recommendations, the federal government adopted its multiculturalism policy in 1971. One objective of that policy was to encourage immigrants to learn at least one of Canada's two official languages to help them become full-fledged members of Canadian society.

At the same time, a regional Francophone identity began to be asserted. The 1960s marked the end of the use of the term "French Canadian" as we knew it and the emergence of Franco-Manitobans, Franco-Albertans and Franco-Ontarians, to name just a few.[6] In 1969, the *Association canadienne française*

---

[4] Office of the French Language Services Commissioner. 2012. *The State of French-Language Postsecondary Education in Central-Southwestern Ontario: No Access, No Future*, Investigation Report. Toronto, ON: Office of the French Language Services Commissioner.

[5] Laurendeau-Dunton Commission. 1969. *The Cultural Contribution of the Other Ethnic Groups*, Volume 4.

[6] Michel Bock and Gaétan Gervais. 2004. *L'Ontario français: Des Pays-d'en-Haut à nos jours*. Toronto, ON: Centre francoontarien de ressources pédagogiques, p. 183.

de l'Ontario (ACFO) boycotted the Estates General of French Canada, thus confirming the end of the solidarity of the French Canadian family.[7]

The unfurling of the Franco-Ontarian flag in 1975 reinforced the community's ownership of its cultural and linguistic identity in the province. This was the start of constructing a pluralistic social vision of a French-speaking community in Ontario.

In 2009, the Ontario government's adoption of the Inclusive Definition of Francophone (IDF), which was a first in Canada, added a building block to the pluralistic structure that characterizes the present day Franco-Ontarian population.

Beyond the natural and foreseeable impact of such a redefinition on statistical data, the IDF above all officially recognized members of ethno-cultural communities as Francophones in the province, thus strengthening their sense of belonging in the Franco-Ontarian community – an increasingly diverse community sustained by a growing number of Francophone newcomers.

The IDF also applies to exogamous families, who are very much in the majority in Ontario, since many of the children of such couples attend French-language schools. However, they identify more readily with two or even three communities. There are also Francophiles, true natural allies of Francophones, who value linguistic duality and see it as an asset for their children and for Ontario society in general.

In this demographic mosaic, accents and dialects from here and elsewhere exist alongside the words people use to define themselves: French Canadian, Franco-Ontarian, Francophone from Ontario, Francophone Canadian or even bilingual, as studies on youth identity show. This diversity can sometimes lead to the borrowing of a few English expressions, but this is hardly an awkward situation.

In short, there is no question that the Laurendeau-Dunton Commission had an indelible impact. Not only did it shape the

---

[7] Gaétan Gervais 1999. "L'histoire de l'*Ontario français (16101997)*" in Joseph Yvon Thériault (ed.). *Francophonies minoritaires au Canada — L'état des lieux.* Moncton, NB: Éditions d'Acadie, p. 157.

country's legal and linguistic landscape with the enactment of French language services legislation in Ontario, Nova Scotia and Prince Edward Island, but it also paved the way for what was to be a multicultural society within a bilingual framework, thereby contributing to the shared foundation of living together in Canada.

Ontario's Francophone community can now rely on tangible progress and count on the presence of institutions and establishments to grow and flourish. However, the challenges are numerous, and minorities will never have the power of the majority. As a result, the protection of their legislative and constitutional rights will always be necessary to maintain the linguistic duality and cultural diversity that are characteristic of Canada.

5

A Manitoban Perspective on the B and B Commission[1]

Roger Turenne

The Laurendeau-Dunton Commission was created in July 1963. The summer of 1963 was also the summer I had my first job, which was as a tour guide at the Legislative Building, the first position that was officially designated bilingual in Manitoba's public service.

The Royal Commission on Bilingualism and Biculturalism (B and B Commission) was set up by Prime Minister Pearson to deal with the awakening of French Canada. My tour guide position was created by Manitoba Premier Duff Roblin because he found it absurd that a third of Canadians could not tour the seat of government in their own language.

These were two events, one much more modest than the other, that marked the start of the long journey of bilingualism in Manitoba over the past 50 years. The B and B Commission had a very profound effect on Manitoba, mainly because of its impact on the Francophone community and the ripple effect it had on provincial governments.

In 1963, Manitoba's Francophone community was in a state of crisis, as noted in the B and B Commission's 1965 interim report, which talked about the critical situation of Francophone

[1] Paper presented at Université de Saint-Boniface as part of a symposium celebrating the 50th anniversary of the Royal Commission on Bilingualism and Biculturalism, April 16, 2013.

minorities outside of Quebec. The assimilation of young people was occurring at a pace that suggested that the community would disappear in the not too distant future.

There were several causes: the fact that instruction had become almost entirely in English in the 1950s, urbanization, the consolidation of school divisions, the advent of television, the explosion of rock music, and exogamous marriages.

All of this was in a context in which the *Public Schools Act* prohibited not only the use of French as a language of instruction but also the teaching of the French language before Grade 4.[2]

The community was also deeply divided in three ways:

1. the division between those who were comfortable with the status quo and hesitated to rock the boat, and those who wanted to make demands more aggressively and take the risks that had to be taken given the seriousness of the situation;

2. the division between those whose priority was assisting Catholic private schools and those who advocated non-denominational French public schools; and

3. the division between those who advocated bilingual schools and those who saw entirely French schools as the only solution.

The Commission came along at just the right time and played an important role in the outcome of these three conflicts.

Inspired by the sort of *glasnost* that the Commission represented, the supporters of militancy in French Manitoba rather quickly overcame the timorous.

The second major conflict, between the supporters of Catholic private schools and the supporters of French public schools, was more difficult to resolve. In the early 1960s, Manitoba Francophones identified as Catholic French Canadians and not Franco-Manitobans – a term that did not come into existence until the end of the decade.

The community's institutions reflected this religious heritage and were no longer equal to the challenge at hand. Even

[2] Paul-Émile Leblanc. 1968. *L'enseignement du français au Manitoba, 1916-1968.* Master's thesis. Ottawa, ON: University of Ottawa.

the community's main organization, the *Association d'éducation des Canadiens français du Manitoba* (AECFM), had difficulty drawing a line between language and religion.

One of the main tools in the AECFM's transformation into the *Société franco-manitobaine* (SFM) was a process of social action, awareness and public participation that culminated in the rally of French Manitoba in 1968. This process played a crucial role in the declericalization of the community.[3]

But an endeavour of such scope cost money. For the first time in history, funds were available from the federal government. Why? Because the B and B Commission, in its preliminary report in 1965, had shed light on the crisis faced by minority communities and the key role they had to play in strengthening Canadian unity.

The result was an assistance program for minorities under which Manitoba was one of the first and largest recipients. Because of the small demographic weight of Franco-Manitobans and the magnitude of the challenges to be met, that community needed a very strong institutional structure that only outside financial support could ensure.

Next came the *Official Languages Act,*[4] which arose out of the Laurendeau-Dunton Commission's recommendations. In addition to giving Francophone minorities a sense of pride and courage in making their demands, the Act also had a ripple effect on certain provincial governments, which, with the incentive of federal funds, may have been inclined to think that communicating with their constituents in French was not as risky as it used to be.

But the provincial governments still needed receptive leaders with a minimum of vision and courage.

Over the past 50 years, with the very brief exception of 19 months (1967-1969) under the unfortunate Walter Weir, Manitoba has been extremely fortunate to have had premiers who have all been sympathetic to the cause of bilingualism and who have often been enlightened and sometimes even courageous.

---

[3] On this point, see *"Le Rallye du Manitoba français"* in Raymond Hebert. 2012. *La Révolution tranquille au Manitoba français*. Winnipeg, MB: Éditions du Blé, chapter 5.
[4] *Official Languages Act of Canada*, R.S.C. 1970, c. 0-1.

There was Duff Roblin, a visionary recognized as the greatest of Manitobans, who was the first to change a situation that had been static for more than 40 years with regard to the status of French in schools: first by allowing French to be taught in public schools starting in Grade 1 and then, for the first time in half a century, by reinstating French as a language of instruction for up to 50 percent of classes.

There was Ed Schreyer, who threw open the door that had been half opened by Roblin, and to whom we owe entirely French schools, the *Bureau de l'éducation française* (BEF), the *Centre culturel franco-manitobain* (CCFM) and the *Institut pédagogique*. There had never been anything like it in all·of Manitoba's history.

Next came Sterling Lyon. Some will be surprised to see him on a list of premiers who were Francophiles – or at least open to the expansion of Francophone space – given his virulent opposition to the proposed constitutional amendment in 1983. But that was the embittered Sterling in the Opposition. I am focusing here only on his actions as Premier.

Lyon had the misfortune of being in office at the time of the Supreme Court's decision in the Forest case.[5] It is difficult to imagine today how that decision may have shocked Manitoba society, especially since the Court gave no direction for remedying the constitutional affront it had just revealed.

Despite a false start with the passage of the infamous *Bill 2*, Sterling Lyon nonetheless chose to go beyond the minimum requirements of section 23[6] and develop a policy for services in French. He also hired a special advisor to develop such a policy.

Eighteen years after I started as a tour guide at the Legislative Building, I returned to the same building to undertake a task that would have seemed completely improbable in 1963. A few months later, the Lyon government was defeated and replaced by Howard Pawley's government.

---

[5] *Forest v. Attorney General of Manitoba*, [1979] 1 S.C.R. 1032.

[6] Section of the *Manitoba Act, 1870*, which requires the bilingual enactment of statutes and bilingualism in the courts; not to be confused with the other section 23, of the Canadian Charter, which deals with language of instruction.

It was under Pawley's leadership that services in French truly began in Manitoba. It was also under his leadership that the disastrous attempt to amend the Constitution to entrench the right to such services was made.

I do not want to go into detail about that episode, but there is one thing to remember about the Pawley government – the solidarity of all but two members of the NDP caucus despite the turmoil and the prospect of near certain electoral defeat if it saw its proposal through to the end, which it was prepared to do had it not been for the SFM, which asked it to give up, rightly believing that it was better to go to the Supreme Court[7] than to have an imperfect statute enacted in a poisoned atmosphere.

Defeat came anyway four years later, and Conservative Gary Filmon came to office. The Franco-Manitoban community was not very enthusiastic about the change. The killer of entrenchment was now in power. A year later, at my suggestion, the SFM invited the Premier to speak at its annual meeting.

Imagine how surprised the audience was to hear the man who had rung the bells seven years earlier formally commit to a program to actively offer services in French! And what can be said of the commitment to extend services in French to hospitals – which even NDP Minister of Health Laurent Desjardins, a Francophone, had refused to consider!

It was under Gary Filmon that the *Division scolaire franco-manitobaine* (DSFM) was established. And when the implementation of the policy began to stall, he commissioned the Chartier report, which led to the creation of bilingual service centres.[8] Not a bad track record, really.

The Doer and Selinger years were marked by the extension and consolidation of services in French and the expansion of Francophone space in the economy, municipalities and immigration.

---

[7] The Court found that Manitoba had to translate and reenact all its statutes in both languages: statutes enacted in English only were unconstitutional: *Re Manitoba Language Rights*, [1985] 1 S.C.R. 783.

[8] Richard Chartier. 1998. *Above All, Common Sense: Report and Recommendations on French Language Services Within the Government of Manitoba*. http://www.gov. mb.ca/fls-slf/report/pdf/toc.html (consulted on February 11, 2014).

For more than 20 years now, bilingualism in government in Manitoba has been part of a broad consensus both in the political sphere and among what might be called the elite of Manitoba society. It is a consensus that originated with the creation of the B and B Commission half a century earlier.

6.

Bilingualism in Canada: Challenges for the Future[1]

Raymond-M. Hébert

To be able to propose future paths for the development of bilingualism in Canada, we must first know where we came from and, above all, we must have analytical tools that make it possible to determine where we should be in the fairly well-defined future. I am proposing here, as a starting point, a macrocosmic view that will enable us to identify the achievements and shortcomings of Canadian bilingualism.

Montreal lawyer Ingride Roy has developed an analytical framework involving three stages or levels of bilingualism.[2] According to Ms. Roy, in international law, the state must ensure that minorities within its territory can speak their languages and preserve their traditions and customs. This occurs on a personal and private level. At the second stage or, if one prefers, the second level, the state must protect minorities and help them maintain their languages and cultures. In Canada, the state makes constant choices about minorities, which means that the status of one type of minority in relation to another is in constant

[1] Paper presented at Université de Saint-Boniface as part of a symposium celebrating the 50th anniversary of the Royal Commission on Bilingualism and Biculturalism, April 16, 2013.

[2] Ingride Roy, presentation entitled *"Les droits linguistiques et les droits des minorités linguistiques en droit international"* for a course on language rights in Canada offered by the Faculty of Law, University of Manitoba, April 3, 2013.

flux. Being Aboriginal or a member of a Francophone minority or Ukrainian or black is not the same thing under the laws, funding and programs of the Canadian government. Ms. Roy calls this level protective bilingualism, which is centred around rights to protection. For our purposes, we will focus solely on official language minorities.

Third, once protective bilingualism is ensured, it becomes necessary to consider the state's obligation to pass legislation or take other measures to secure the right of minorities to participate, or what can be called participative bilingualism. It is this level that is the least developed in Canada as far as Francophone minorities are concerned. We can define participative bilingualism as a situation in which the linguistic minority has an opportunity to participate not only in the development of laws affecting it but also in the resulting governance institutions.

There are plenty of examples of protective bilingualism. First, there is the modern development of French schools starting in the 1950s, first with French classes offered at school, then the teaching of certain classes (the socalled 50/50 model), then the creation of entirely French public schools and, finally, the establishment of a Franco-Manitoban school division in 1994. Mention can also be made of the provision of provincial services in French, which is a good example of the right to speak French extending from the private to the public arena. There is also the creation of the *Centre culturel franco-manitobain*, which helps protect the rights of the official minority to maintain and develop its culture. Finally, there is the establishment of Francophone public media (radio and television), again with the goal of maintaining and encouraging the development of the French language and culture.[3]

Participative bilingualism goes much further. According to Ms. Roy, this type of bilingualism implies that members of the minority can "play an effective part in decisions that concern them or that concern the areas where they live." It is therefore necessary to "ensure the participation of members of minority

[3] Three websites summarize the history of French Manitoba and the development of its institutions. See http://www.sfm.mb.ca/communaute/histoire_du_manitoba_francais/, http://www.sfm.mb.ca/centre-info-233-allo/centre_de_ressources/ and http://shsb.mb.ca/en/node/354.

communities in cultural, religious, social, economic and public life" and, finally, to "ensure their full participation in their country's economic development and progress (our emphasis)."[4]

Using the elements of this definition as an analytical framework, we will begin by noting the gains made by French Manitoba with this type of bilingualism. Some of the gains date back to the 1960s and 1970s. One example is the structural participation of Manitoban Francophones in the public school system, which is stronger than ever in its modern iteration. In the Manitoba Teachers' Society, an organization representing all Manitoban teachers, *éducatrices et éducateurs francophones du Manitoba*, has an important voice. The Manitoba School Boards Association, in which the *Division scolaire franco-manitobaine* participates, has direct ties with and an important influence on the Minister of Education.[5]

In modern times, that is, since the 1980s and 1990s, many other 'gains' have been made by French Manitoba as a result of the hard work of certain Francophone leaders, and all of the gains are consistent with participative bilingualism. One example is the Association of Manitoba's Bilingual Municipalities (AMBM): the AMBM's 17 municipalities include official language minority communities in which the use of French is recognized as an added value in economic, social and cultural terms.[6] The association facilitates linkages and gives the minority a direct influence on municipal decision makers, for example with the current movement, in 2013, toward the amalgamation of municipalities, which involves adjustments to bilingualism at the local level.

Another important example is the Economic Development Council for Manitoba Bilingual Municipalities (CDEM).[7] Created in 1996, CDEM is the driving force behind economic

---

[4] Ingride Roy, presentation entitled *"Les droits linguistiques et les droits des minorités linguistiques en droit international"* for a course on language rights in Canada offered by the Faculty of Law, University of Manitoba, April 3, 2013.

[5] For the DSFM, see https://www.dsfm.mb.ca/; for the ÉFM, see http://www.efm-mts.org/?page_id=138; for the School Boards Association, see http://www.mbschoolboards.ca/.

[6] See http://directionmanitoba.com/en/.

[7] See http://www.cdem.com/en.

development in Manitoba's 17 bilingual municipalities. Its mission is to stimulate, encourage, support and coordinate economic development in the AMBM's communities. CDEM initiated Manitoba's Bilingual Trade Agency (ANIM),[8] a bilingual agency served by Francophone staff, which develops and maintains direct ties with Manitoba's private and public economic decision makers. ANIM in turn led to the Centrallia organization, which has its roots in the internationally renowned Futurallia forum, which has connected thousands of businesses around the world since it was established in 1990. The Centrallia event took place in Winnipeg in 2012;[9] it facilitated economic linkages between Manitoba Francophones and the international business community. In 2012, ANIM became one of the main partners in a new bilingual World Trade Centre in Winnipeg, which, among other things, strengthens ties between Manitoba's Francophones and Anglophones in the business sector and with governments.[10]

In the health-care field, the St. Boniface Health Centre[11] has been providing numerous medical and other services in both languages for many years now. It was established by Université de Saint-Boniface, the Catholic Health Corporation of Manitoba and the *Société franco-manitobaine*. Led by an entirely Francophone board of directors, it has a staff of about 30 people and serves as one way for Manitoban Francophones to make their voices heard by institutions like the St. Boniface General Hospital and the provincial Department of Health.

Despite the rapid development of these institutions (these "mechanisms of participative bilingualism" for the purposes of our presentation), there is always a possibility of losing ground. For example, federal or provincial budget cuts can slow down or even reverse advances in both protective and participative bilingualism. A few recent examples: the reduction in Service Canada activities at the St. Boniface Bilingual Service Centre (from five days to two days) in 2012 as a result of budget cuts by the Harper government, and cuts to funding for Riel House

---

[8] See http://news.gov.mb.ca/news/?item=12944.
[9] See http://www.centrallia.com/.
[10] See http://www.wtcwinnipeg.com/.
[11] See http://www.centredesante.mb.ca/index.php?lang=en.

in St. Vital, a historic site in memory of Louis Riel.[12] A more striking and potentially much more serious example is the recent elimination (2012) of the provincial role in managing the Provincial Nominee Program in the immigration context. Close ties had been developed between the province, ANIM and *Accueil francophone* in managing this program, under which about 7 percent of the immigrants welcomed to the province each year were Francophone.

For the future, I believe that the main challenge for the Franco-Manitoban community, and I suspect for other Francophone minority communities as well, is to counter a certain sense of lost momentum, if not apathy. Because of all the gains made in the past few decades, starting in particular with the Charter of Rights and Freedoms in 1982 and everything that followed, there is sometimes an impression that everything has already been won. However, as we have said, these gains are sometimes fragile, since they continue to depend in part on the goodwill of governments, especially in the case of funding. I would therefore emphasize, first and foremost, the need to revitalize Manitoba's Francophone community. One way would be a change of leadership, particularly in the *Société franco-manitobaine*, which has not been known for making political demands lately, even though this is its primary mandate. A second way would be to restore a sense of pride that seems to have disappeared from public discourse. I have floated the idea of a large rally every five years, similar to the congresses or rallies of old, that would attract hundreds if not thousands of Manitoban Francophones. This could be done by planning the annual general meetings of all the organizations of Manitoba's *Francophonie* for a single weekend in a single location. It would simultaneously be a place of work (regular sessions of each organization individually), assembly (pooling of all these plans) and social and cultural celebration. We could even consider coordinating such an event with the five-year planning of the Roadmap for Francophone communities by the Department of Canadian Heritage.

---

[12] See http://shsb.mb.ca/en/riel_house.

In short, our challenges are very different today because of all the gains that have been made in priority areas since the end of the 1960s, both with protective bilingualism and with participative bilingualism. In Manitoba, just like everywhere else in Canada for minority communities, priority was given to these areas on the heels of the work of the Royal Commission on Bilingualism and Biculturalism. However, there is still a great deal to accomplish, especially with participative bilingualism and the revitalization of Francophone communities in the 21st century.

7

Official Bilingualism: Fair Exchange?[1]

Sherry Simon

Official bilingualism in Canada, one of the principal recommendations of the Royal Commission on Bilingualism and Biculturalism (B and B Commission), is a noble ideal. It is also a successful reality within the limits of its mandate: to ensure that the government and governmental services speak two languages to its citizens. Official bilingualism gives us moral high ground: our southern neighbours, who are as multilingual as we are, see no advantage in giving legal rights or national recognition to Spanish. It also gives us international prestige: Canada has developed a massive and well-oiled translation machine that is admired worldwide. Translators are rarely given the credit they deserve and official bilingualism relies much more than most realize on the hidden work of translation. Training and research in the burgeoning field of Translation Studies and Terminology have put Canada on the map for specialists all around the world.

But any feelings of collective self-satisfaction should be tempered by the realities on the ground. Bilingualism is a

[1] Paper given at the conference on *"Est-ce que le bilinguisme a un avenir au Canada,"* held at McGill University May 1, 2013 in the context of the celebrations surrounding the 50th anniversary of the Royal Commission on Bilingualism and Biculturalism.

very partial recognition of the differences in Canadian society. It privileges a single axis of Canadian identity, and largely relegates questions of First Nations and immigrant language and identity to other areas of jurisdiction. While we are aware of what bilingualism allows Canadian society to do, there is far less awareness of the needs of these communities.[2] How could the kinds of success that official bilingualism has given French in Canada be extended to other important constituencies of Canadian society? This is a legitimate and pressing question.

Equally importantly, though official bilingualism aims to guarantee legal equality between French and English, it functions through profound inequality. Official bilingualism helps to perpetuate a fictional idea of language relations – the fiction of symmetry that we see on cereal boxes and government brochures, the mirror-image paragraphs that show English and French as absolutely equal. In fact, given that most of government documents begin in English and are translated into French, the lion's share of translation goes into French. (I have informally heard the figure of 90 percent but figures are not available for confirmation). This means that most ideas and policies are conceived in English, then brought over into French. And so there has been an unevenness at the heart of official bilingualism from the start – a lack of symmetry that helps explain why Anglophones and Francophones have differing perceptions of bilingualism. For a strong and confident language, translation is an act of generosity and inclusion. For a fragile language, translation can be threatening: the weaker language becomes a repository of realities generated in another milieu. And a long tradition of mediocre translation[3] – now largely corrected – instilled a suspicion of translation in Francophone culture. Translation carried out under official bilingualism carries a baggage of inequality beneath the

---

[2] For instance, see Ellen Gabriel's comments on language needs for First Nations: https://sovereignvoices1.wordpress.com/2012/09/02/language-laws-and-the-threat-to-onkwehonwe-indigenous-languages-quebec-election-issues/.

[3] See my *L'inscription sociale de la traduction au Québec* (Editeur officiel, Gouvernement du Québec, Collection Langues et sociétés, 1989), which documents awareness of and resistance to 'bad' translation during the 1950s and 1960s.

scrupulously doubled surfaces of government documents, web pages, labels and notices.

Official bilingualism should not deceive us into thinking that we are multilingual and therefore open to the world. In the field of literary translation, for instance, we need to be much more open to other languages and to widen the application of our considerable expertise. Canadians have become skilled in translating to each other. Canadian literary translation since the 1970s has created entire libraries of literature in the other language. First there was a great wave of translation from French into English; now there is an equally important movement from English into French – as can be seen in the catalogues of major Quebec literary publishers like Boréal and Leméac. Canadian translations are now published in New York and in Paris, no longer considered purely local products. Here again, Canadians are admired for the quantity and quality of work that is produced – for the prominence that some of our translators have achieved, the honours they have received, the support they are given by publishers and government programs. But paradoxically, 'our' two languages can close us off from the world, confining the great mass of literary translation work to the Canadian scene. This is because of the structure of the financing programs of the Canada Council, and because of the colonial heritage which privileges publishers from Paris or New York over those of Toronto or Montreal. Canadian translators should also see themselves as translators of the world – as open to French and Francophone literature as Quebec writing, as open to the Spanish of Latin America and the Arabic of North Africa. But they need access to the international translation market.

We need to be open to the changing nature of language interactions in everyday life. Bilingualism is never symmetrical: for individuals as for cities, transactions between languages never come out exactly even. Montreal is not a bilingual city, if by that it is suggested an idea of fair and symmetrical exchange. Montreal today is a Francophone city where English and French enter into a conversation whose terms are continually changing. What is changing most is the status of English. Less and less the language of a historically rooted community, English is increasingly a diverse, international language spoken by locals and newcomers. It is no longer possible to use the label Anglophone – or Francophone – with total confidence. The lawyer and human rights activist Julius Grey writes that he doesn't consider himself an Anglophone but *"un Québécois qui parle français et anglais."*[4] The community which once claimed to speak with one voice in provincial politics no longer makes such a claim. The Anglophone community is now much too diverse and too intermingled with the Francophone community to define itself as one unit. Mixed marriages and mixed neighbourhoods are generating new idioms, some of them indeed 'mixed up'. But the dangers of too much contact seem minor compared to the damage inflicted by isolation.

To recognize the profoundly different cultural forces that meet through practices of translation in Canada does not mean, however, that official bilingualism should be scrapped. *Au contraire.* The Harper administration is looking for ways to dismantle the public institutions that have been so important to Canadians over the years – the railways, the CBC, arts funding, and the list goes on. Canada needs the *Official Languages Act* – while recognizing its limitations. And some must renew our commitment to institutional bilingualism and oppose the constant erosion of government support for programs and offices like the Translation Bureau. The federal government relies increasingly on outsourcing for translation and has largely withdrawn from training activities. While most translators were once employed in the public sector, today only 17 percent of the 15,000 translators are public sector employees.[5]

[4] http://www.ledevoir.com/politique/quebec/359290/l-anglais-un-atout-pour-tous-les-quebecois.

[5] *Translation Bureau Benchmarking and Comparative Analysis,* May 15, 2012: http://www.bt-tb.tpsgc-pwgsc.gc.ca/publications/documents/rapport-report-benchmarking-eng.pdf.

Official bilingualism is necessary, necessary but not sufficient. It is one way in which Canadian reality is expressed, and this way has become essential to the integration of Quebec within the Canadian federation. Federal official bilingualism should be defended not as an expression of a superior humanistic culture or as a form of altruism, but as a strategic recognition of Francophone minorities across the country as well as Quebec national identity into a now fully integrated understanding of citizenship.

Bilingual *and* multicultural? Canada's two cultural policies seem to belong to parallel universes. Any assessment of official bilingualism must recognize the real tensions between these different visions of the country as well as the constituencies they both ignore. But while official bilingualism can be criticized for proposing a façade of equality where none exists, it must be defended against the current government's undermining of public institutions.

8.

The Legacy of the Laurendeau-Dunton Commission and The Principle of Cultural Equality[1]

Michelle Landry

Considering the legacy of an event is always a difficult process since direct consequential relationships are rare in the unfolding of history. In the case of the Royal Commission on Bilingualism and Biculturalism, many of the recommendations were never even adopted, including the centrepiece of the report, the creation of bilingual districts. The fact remains that other important events followed the Commission, and the debates it generated and the ideas it put forward justify speaking unequivocally of a legacy.

Without question, the official bilingualism and multiculturalism policies are one of the most important aspects of the legacy of the Commission on Bilingualism and Biculturalism.[2] Yet language rights in Canada were adopted

---

[1] Paper presented as part of the celebrations marking the 50th anniversary of the Royal Commission on Bilingualism and Biculturalism at Université de Moncton, June 14, 2013.

[2] Jack Jedwab. 2003. "To 'Bi' and not to 'Bi': Canada's Royal Commission on Bilingualism and Biculturalism, 1960-1980," *Canadian Issues / Thèmes canadiens,* June, p. 19-22.

by Pierre E. Trudeau's government from a liberal perspective, giving precedence to individual rights and thereby, in a sense, ignoring the question of biculturalism.[3] There is not enough space here to discuss how the Trudeau government, which adopted these policies, and the commissioners, particularly Laurendeau, differed in their views on the law and language and cultural issues. However, we note that the Commission's position was based on the idea of two founding peoples and sought to find a way to change course to achieve equality between these two peoples for whom language was the defining characteristic. It will be recalled that the Commission's terms of reference were in fact:

> to inquire into and report upon the existing state of bilingualism and biculturalism in Canada and to recommend what steps should be taken to develop the Canadian Confederation on the basis of an equal partnership between the two founding races, taking into account the contribution made by the other ethnic groups to the cultural enrichment of Canada and the measures that should be taken to safeguard that contribution.[4]

The Commission proposed a new articulation of this national endeavour based on the idea of nonterritorial cultural duality while advancing the concept of cultural equality that ran through all of its work. According to sociologist Simon Langlois,[5] this concept was promptly forgotten at the end of the Commission's work, since the Trudeau government categorically rejected this concept of cultural equality in order to emphasize individual equality. As well, the multiculturalism policy obscured the idea of cultural duality as an extension of the idea of founding peoples. Some may see this as a minor detail, but the fact is that, in New Brunswick, this concept of cultural equality was and still is a key concept in the claims and rights of Acadians.

---

[3] The courts have since introduced a collective dimension to language rights. See, inter alia, Mahe v. Alberta, [1990] 1 S.C.R. 372.

[4] Royal Commission on Bilingualism and Biculturalism. 1967. Report of the Royal Commission on Bilingualism and Biculturalism, General Introduction, Book I: The Official Languages, p. xxi.

[5] Simon Langlois. 2003. "Le biculturalisme oublié," Canadian Issues / Thèmes canadiens, June, p. 27-29.

In the remainder of this text, we will briefly trace the history of the main administrative arrangements, laws, language rights and cultural rights that apply in New Brunswick to show how they relate to the concept of cultural equality put forward by the Laurendeau-Dunton Commission. What we would like to suggest here is that the enactment of language laws must be understood in light of the typical process of legitimating government action through the law. As Duran[6] notes, the law and bureaucracy, which are components of rational-legal domination as defined by Weber, remain legitimate even in the current context in which governance goes far beyond the traditional state and several forms of power are outside the state. Power relationships exist wherever one group is subordinate to another and normalized identities are challenged, and not only in relationships with the state.[7]

However, [translation] "the state remains the key political player in society and the most prominent expression of the collective interest",[8] or at least of a certain political and societal compromise. The state therefore finds legitimacy in the exercise of power in accordance with the law. The fact remains that the state is continually building and transforming itself, for example by enacting new laws based on the consequences of social mobilization and struggles, whether or not they lead to challenges and demands.[9] In other words, we would argue that the Laurendeau-Dunton Commission influenced militant discourse and demands, and gave legitimacy to some strictly political actions, that is, the actions of governments, including the enactment of legislation. In fact, not only was its influence felt while it carried out its terms of reference, but its legacy is still very present today, especially in New Brunswick, where the principle of cultural equality is institutionalized, including in the *Act Recognizing the Equality of the Two Linguistic Communities*[10]

---

[6] Patrice Duran. 2009. "Légitimité, droit et action publique," *L'Année sociologique*, 59 (2): 303-344.

[7] Kate Nash. 2010. *Contemporary Political Sociology: Globalization, Politics, and Power*, 2nd ed. Chichester, UK: Willey-Blackwell.

[8] P. Duran, *op.cit.*, p. 323.

[9] K. Nash, *op.cit.*

[10] *An Act Recognizing the Equality of the Two Official Linguistic Communities*, R.S.N.B. c. 0-1.1.

and section 16.1 of the Canadian Charter of Rights and Freedoms, which guarantees the equality of the province's two linguistic communities and their right to manage their institutions, including their cultural institutions.[11]

The Laurendeau-Dunton Commission worked during a pivotal time in Acadia, when new forms of language claims and demands for recognition were supplanting the old ones[12] and a new class of players was developing, made up of young people who were increasingly educated.[13] Until that time, the Acadian elite had acted by exerting a discreet influence, particularly through the *Ordre de Jacques Cartier* and other organizations and associations. The language crisis described by the Laurendeau-Dunton Commission mainly involved the relationship between Francophone Quebecers and Anglophones in the rest of Canada, but the national affirmation movement that took shape in Quebec obviously influenced Francophones in the other provinces. In Acadia, starting with the student movement in 1968 and 1969, demands were increasingly made publicly and without restraint.

When the first report of the Royal Commission on Bilingualism and Biculturalism was tabled in 1967, the Liberal government of Louis J. Robichaud (1960-1970) was in the middle of tax and municipal reforms as part of its Equal Opportunity Program. The province's Legislative Assembly had also adopted the principle of two official languages a few months earlier, but the government, well aware of the Laurendeau-Dunton Commission's work, waited for the Commission's first report before tabling a first motion on official languages, just as it waited for the federal Act to be enacted before it passed

---

[11] Enacted in 1993, section 16.1 of the Canadian Charter, in addition to recognizing collective rights, imposes an obligation on the provincial government to promote this equality between the communities.

[12] Michelle Landry. 2011. *La question du politique en Acadie. Les transformations de l'organisation sociopolitique des Acadiens du Nouveau-Brunswick.* Doctoral thesis. Laval, QC: Université de Laval.

[13] Louis F. Cimino. 1977. *Ethnic Nationalism Among the Acadians of New Brunswick: An Analysis of Ethnic Political Development.* Doctoral thesis. Durham, NC: Duke University.

the provincial Act.[14] In the 1970s, the Conservative government of Richard Hatfield (19701987) enacted the remaining sections of the *Official Languages Act* and restructured the Department of Education to achieve what is now called linguistic duality in that department. That government also passed the *Act Recognizing the Equality of the Two Official Linguistic Communities in New Brunswick*,[15] a declaratory statute that contains no legal remedies[16] but is essentially of symbolic importance because of what it recognizes. The power represented by control over an institution, like the educational system, made Acadian militants confident that there were certainly other spheres of activity or government institutions that could be divided up based on the same principle. The principle of cultural equality and the right to manage their institutions, therefore, became central to their demands.

In fact, the language provisions adopted during the 1960s and 1970s were the result of political games[17] between various players, including members of the government, such as Premier Hatfield and his "Acadian lieutenant," Jean-Maurice Simard, Acadian militants who were members of the SANB and the *Parti acadien*, and other players from various organizations or the field of education. For example, later in the early 1990s, following the failure of the Meech Lake and Charlottetown negotiations, the New Brunswick government led by Frank McKenna and the federal government led by Brian Mulroney agreed to entrench in the Constitution the principle of equality of both linguistic communities and their right to manage their cultural institutions (section 16.1).

---

[14] *Official Languages of New Brunswick Act*, R.S.N.B. c. O1. See Robert Pichette. 2001. "Culture and Official Languages" in *The Robichaud Era, 1960-70 - Colloquium Proceedings*. Moncton, NB: Canadian Institute for Research on Regional Development.

[15] *An Act Recognizing the Equality of the Two Official Linguistic Communities in New Brunswick*, S.N.B. c. O-1.1.

[16] Pierre Foucher. 2012. "Autonomie des communautés francophones minoritaires du Canada: le point de vue du droit," *Linguistic Minorities and Society / Minorités linguistiques et société*, p. 103.

[17] See M. Landry, 2011, *op.cit.*

Although this section has been clearly raised in just one case,[18] we can say that its existence has led to certain negotiations to prevent administrative restructuring that would have been detrimental to the Acadians' power of self-determination, a little like a sword of Damocles hanging over the leaders' heads. Examples include the amalgamation of Dieppe with Moncton and Riverview, and the reform of health authorities.[19]

In short, the law plays an important role when it comes to the need to recognize the country's linguistic minorities. In a plural setting like Canada and especially New Brunswick, it is difficult to identify shared visions or a general interest, so [translation] "rules of law provide an effective mechanism for managing social relationships once a compromise must be reached."[20] Rules of law are based on principles and fit within ideologies or even visions of the world. The concept of equality among cultural groups, which the Laurendeau-Dunton Commission held dear and which is an extension of the idea of two founding peoples, has by no means disappeared from ideologies, since it forms the basis for the legitimization of many linguistic demands, including in education and health, and certain government actions, such as the enactment of the *Act Recognizing the Equality of the Two Official Linguistic Communities* in New Brunswick and section 16.1 of the Canadian Charter of Rights and Freedoms.

---

[18] Michel Doucet. 2013. "L'article 16.1 ou comment on en est arrivé à reconnaître la spécificité du Nouveau-Brunswick," *Colloque Égalité et autonomie: le passé, le présent et l'avenir de l'article 16.1* Moncton, NB : Université de Moncton, March 16.

[19] P. Foucher, *op.cit.*

[20] P. Duran, *op.cit.*, p. 315.

9.

The Impact of Book IV of the *Report of the Commission on Bilingualism and Biculturalism* on Fundamental Rights and Multiculturalism in Canada[1]

Ingride Roy

Introduction

The *Royal Commission on Bilingualism and Biculturalism*, also called the Laurendeau-Dunton Commission, was established in 1963 by the federal government. For nearly seven years, it considered the issue of the relationship between the country's two founding peoples but also a variety of issues related to the future of French-Canadian identity and the contribution made by other ethnic groups to the cultural enrichment of Canada. In the end, the Commission published its report and made recommendations in six separate books.

In this text, we will look specifically at the impact of Book IV of the report, "The Cultural Contribution of the Other Ethnic

[1] This text was written for the symposium entitled "The Commission on Bilingualism and Biculturalism Fifty Years Later" organized by the University of Ottawa's Faculty of Law, in conjunction with the Official Languages and Bilingualism Institute and the Centre for Continuing Education, in the context of the National Metropolis Conference held on March 13, 2013 in Ottawa.

Groups" (groups of non-British and non-French descent). We will begin with a brief overview of the Commission's findings and then try to identify the impact of the report on the development of the multiculturalism policy in Canada and the adoption of fundamental rights in various legal instruments in the country.

The Commission's findings in Book IV

From the outset, the Commission's terms of reference were twofold:

1. "to inquire into and report upon the existing state of bilingualism and biculturalism in Canada;" and
2. "to recommend what steps should be taken to develop the Canadian confederation on the basis of an equal partnership between the two founding races, taking into account the contribution made by the other ethnic groups to the cultural enrichment of Canada and the measures that should be taken to safeguard that contribution."[2]

The second aspect of the Commission's terms of reference was the focus of Book IV. However, the contribution made by the "other ethnic groups" was considered solely in the context of the co-existence of the two main communities (Anglophones and Francophones) and the recognition of bilingualism and biculturalism. Under its terms of reference, the Commission was not supposed to exhaustively analyze the position of the other ethnic groups in the country, their way of life or their needs, but was instead supposed to explore what these groups could contribute to the two founding societies, on the premise that the dominant cultures could be enriched by contact with other cultures.

The Commission began by identifying these "other ethnic groups" by providing a historical description of immigration in Canada and then looked at the various roles the groups had been able to play in Canadian life. It found that the arrival of newcomers had a definite impact on the Canadian economy

---

[2] *Report of the Royal Commission on Bilingualism and Biculturalism*, Book I – *The Official Languages*. Ottawa, ON: Queen's Printer, 1967, p. xxi, and Book IV – *The Cultural Contribution of the Other Ethnic Groups*. Ottawa, ON: Queen's Printer, 1969, p. 3.

simply by swelling the labour force. Their presence increased the number of workers and added to the pool of experience, talent and expertise in the labour market. It also increased the number of consumers, so merchants could access a larger clientele and keep the economy moving; and it increased the number of taxpayers from whom governments could collect taxes, providing the state with more resources. However, these beneficial effects on the country's economy did not prevent these groups from facing economic struggles, mainly because of the racial discrimination and prejudice suffered by many of them in the employment context.

The Commission also found that newcomers could influence Canadian political life by bringing different viewpoints to political debate as voters, members of political parties and participants in governmental institutions and through the positions they took in the minority press. However, their influence was diminished because they were also discriminated against in this area.

Finally, the Commission found that these groups could play a cultural and social role but that the significance of this role depended on their resistance to assimilation and the extent to which they retained their language and culture. These elements were determined by various factors[3] and varied substantially from one group to another, and "[d]ifferences exist even within the same groups residing in different regions of the country."[4] In Canada as a whole, the Commission also noted the powerful attraction of the English language for people of other than British and French cultural backgrounds and the growing influence of television and the electronic media. On this point, the Commission added that it was difficult to forecast future retention rates for ancestral languages because of the new technological factor, which "may exert an overwhelming influence on … assimilation."[5]

---

[3] The factors identified by the Commission included their number, their rural-urban settlement patterns, their geographic concentration or dispersion, the existence of institutions belonging to the group, their vitality and the presence of first or second generation immigrants in the group.

[4] *Report of the Commission, supra,* note 2, p. 117.

[5] *Ibid.,* p. 135.

The Commission concluded from its inquiry that there was a need to preserve the language and culture of each group in Canada in order to enrich Canadian society. The Commission's focus was, therefore, not on the preservation of the group but rather on its language and culture. It also linked the need to ensure the integration of these other groups with one of the two founding peoples and the protection of the cultures of these other groups to enrich the two dominant cultures. The Commission then found that these cultures could be preserved through certain institutions, including schools, the mass media (such as radio, television and films), and arts and letters.

In short, the Commission recognized that the other ethnic groups could enrich the country's economic, political and social life, but it found that everything was not always in place to recognize or benefit from that contribution.[6] The Commission's recommendations[7] therefore focused mainly on three objectives:

1. integration of the "other ethnic groups" into Canadian society rather than their assimilation;
2. protection of the culture of these "other ethnic groups" so they could integrate better and the two dominant cultures could be enriched; and,
3. recognition for the members of these "other ethnic groups" of all the rights conferred on citizens and their participation in the country's institutions on an equal footing and without discrimination.

---

[6] The following passage from the report clearly expresses the Commission's thoughts on the contribution made by these groups to Canadian society:
"By settling the country [the other ethnic groups] helped to lay the basis for Canada's cultural growth. ... Canadian culture has been the richer for the knowledge, skills, and traditions which all the immigrant groups brought with them. Their many distinctive styles of life gradually increased the range of experience, outlook, ideas, and talents which characterize the country. Cultural diversity has widened our horizons; it has also given opportunities – **not always seized upon** – for various approaches to the solution of our problems" [emphasis added]. *Report of the Commission, supra,* note 2, p. 197.

[7] See the Commission's specific recommendations, *ibid.,* p. 64, 87, 141, 143, 145, 190, 193, 220.

The measures proposed by the Commission to protect these groups and their culture were therefore proposed much more for nation-building purposes than to truly ensure respect for differences or to make it possible for the two main communities (Anglophones and Francophones) to know and interact with these groups.

The influence of Book IV

Book IV of the Commission's report was unquestionably an invaluable tool for the collection of information on the reality of citizens of non-British and non-French origin from the start of Confederation until the time the report was written. It was also an essential starting point for the subsequent preparation of various studies and the creation of working groups on the question of cultural diversity, thereby helping to broaden debate and research on this question. Finally, over the years, it influenced the adoption of legislative and constitutional measures and policies related to language, multiculturalism and protection against discrimination.

With regard to language, Book IV must be read in conjunction with Book I, which urged the recognition of two official languages and influenced the enactment of the *Official Languages Acts* of 1969[8] and 1988,[9] whereas Book IV recognized the richness of the contribution made by other ethnic groups and the importance of protecting their culture and language with the goal of integration into Canadian society. The combination of these two books therefore influenced the adoption of measures to clarify the interaction between the recognition of two official languages and the protection of other languages. These measures included section 38 of the 1969 *Official Languages Act*, section 83 and clause 11 of the preamble of the 1988 *Official Languages Act* and clause 3 of the preamble and paragraphs 3(*i*) and (*j*) of the 1988 *Multiculturalism Act*,[10] all of which provide that official bilingualism should not preclude measures to promote other languages.

[8] *Official Languages Act*, R.S.C. 1970, c. 0-2.
[9] *Official Languages Act*, 1988, c. 38, R.S.C. 1985, c. 31 (4th Supp.).
[10] *Multiculturalism Act*, R.S.C. 1985, c. 24 (4th Supp.).

Book IV also influenced the adoption of a multiculturalism policy in 1971 and the creation of various institutions[11] to implement that policy over the years. It allowed the entrenchment of the principle of multiculturalism in section 27 of the Canadian Charter[12] and the enactment of the *Multiculturalism Act* in 1988.[13]

Finally, Book IV influenced the creation of many government programs to combat racism, hate and prejudice in Canada, the adoption of legislative and constitutional measures dealing with the right to equality and non-discrimination, including the *Canadian Human Rights Act*,[14] provincial legislation concerning rights and freedoms[15] and section 15 of the Canadian Charter, and the enactment of more specific provisions concerning non-discrimination in the exercise of democratic rights[16] and with respect to employment.[17]

---

[11] Including the Multiculturalism Directorate of the Department of the Secretary of State in 1972, the Ministry of State for Multiculturalism and the Canadian Multiculturalism Council (which later became the Canadian Ethnocultural Council) in 1973. Over the years, these various institutions were replaced by other organizations and the implementation of the policy, to which some adjustments were made, was finally entrusted to the Department of Multiculturalism and Citizenship in 1991, the Department of Canadian Heritage in 1993 and, since 2008, the Department of Citizenship and Immigration.

[12] Canadian Charter of Rights and Freedoms, Schedule B to the *Constitution Act, 1982* (U.K.), c. 11, R.S.C. 1985, App. II, No. 44.

[13] The 10 general objectives listed in s. 3 of the *Multiculturalism Act, supra*, note 10, can be summarized as follows: (1) preserving and integrating various cultures while providing equal access to full participation and eliminating racism and discriminatory barriers; (2) promoting institutional change at the federal level to make such participation possible; and (3) taking measures to promote cultural understanding and awareness.

[14] *Canadian Human Rights Act*, R.S.C. 1985, c. H-6.

[15] Including section 10 of the Charter of Human Rights and Freedoms, S.Q. 1975, c. 6, R.S.Q., c. C12, and section 1 of the Ontario Human Rights Code, R.S.O. 1990, c. H-19, but also all provincial human rights legislation.

[16] Including in section 6 of the *Citizenship Act*, R.S.C. 1985, c. C-29.

[17] Including in clause 5 of the preamble to the *OLA, supra*, note 9.

Conclusion

The findings in Book IV of the Report concerning the problems experienced by ethnic groups are still relevant. While the reality and face of immigration have greatly changed and continue to change the landscape of Canadian society, the problems experienced by ethnic groups remain essentially the same. Many members of such groups still face discrimination in various areas of political, economic and social life. The attraction of English still seems to be present for many as well. Indeed, it is particularly unsettling to see how accurate the Commission was at the time in contemplating the overwhelming influence that the electronic media might exert in the future on integration and, to a large extent, on the retention rate for the various ancestral languages of these groups.

The solutions proposed in the report for ending these problems have been implemented almost in their entirety in various legislative and constitutional measures and policies. The measures have not changed much since they were adopted, and most of them are still in effect. It can, therefore, be said that the philosophy of integration-oriented multiculturalism favoured in the report is still very much present today. Ultimately, that policy has introduced a solution with three main aspects:

1. recognition of the contribution made by other ethnic groups and protection of their cultures through specific measures;
2. recognition of the right to equality and protection against discrimination; and,
3. recognition of the importance of measures to foster an understanding of other cultures.

Since the adoption of the multiculturalism policy, there have, of course, been a number of critiques both praising and condemning it.[18] However, regardless of the critiques, and without expressing an opinion on their validity, one fact remains: the policy has not actually resolved everything. To the extent that

[18] For a description of the various critiques, see, *inter alia*: J. Garcea, A. Kirova and L. Wong. 2008. "Multiculturalism Discourses in Canada," *Canadian Ethnic Studies*, 40(1): 110; and M. Labelle. 2008. "Les intellectuels québécois face au multiculturalisme: hétérogénéité des approches et des projets politiques," *Canadian Ethnic Studies*, 40(1): 33-56.

governments would like to preserve the philosophy favoured in the report, it may be asked whether the answers found so far should be changed or at least improved in light of international instruments on "cultural diversity", including the UNESCO Universal Declaration on Cultural Diversity,[19] the Declaration of the Principles of International Cultural Cooperation[20] and certain other instruments adopted to protect minorities.[21]

Each of these international instruments has tried to address the problem of inequalities between groups by including provisions designed not only to protect groups from discrimination and give them specific rights but also to promote tolerance, understanding, cooperation and friendship.[22] These

[19] *UNESCO Universal Declaration on Cultural Diversity*, UNESCO General Conference, 31st Session, November 2, 2001, in K. Sténou and F. de Bernard. 2001. *Déclaration universelle de l'UNESCO sur la diversité culturelle: commentaires et propositions*. Paris, FR: Éditions UNESCO, Cultural Diversity Series No. 2, 158 pages.

[20] *Declaration of the Principles of International Cultural Cooperation*, UNESCO General Conference, 14th Session, November 4, 1966, in *Centre For Human Rights, A Compilation of International Instruments,* Volume I (second part), Universal Instruments. New York, NY and Geneva, Switzerland: United Nations, 1994, p. 591-594.

[21] See, *inter alia*: *United Nations Declaration on the Rights of Persons Belonging to National or Ethnic, Religious and Linguistic Minorities*, in *Centre For Human Rights, A Compilation of International Instruments,* Volume I (second part), Universal Instruments. New York, NY and Geneva, Switzerland: United Nations, 1994, p. 140-143; the *Concluding Document of the 1990 Copenhagen Meeting*, in A. Fenet, G. Koubi, I. Schulte-Tenckhoff and T. Ansbach. 1995. *Le droit et les minorités.* Brussels, BE: Bruylant, p. 399-403; *Framework Convention for the Protection of National Minorities*, November 10, 1994, in P.M. Dupuis. 1996. *Grands textes de droit international public.* Paris, FR: Dalloz, p. 212-221; and the 1990 *Charter of Paris for a New Europe*, in A. Fenet, G. Koubi, I. Schulte-Tenckhoff and T. Ansbach. 1995. *Le droit et les minorités.* Brussels, BE: Bruylant, p. 403-404.

[22] This type of provision can be found both in instruments concerning minorities and in other universal international instruments. For instruments concerning minorities, see, *inter alia*: article 4 of the *Declaration on the Rights of Persons Belonging to National or Ethnic, Religious and Linguistic Minorities, supra*; articles 6 and 14 of the *Council of Europe Framework Convention for the Protection of National Minorities, supra*; and paragraph 34 of the *OSCE's Copenhagen Document, supra*. For other universal international instruments, see also: paragraph 2 of the preamble to the *Charter of the United Nations* on the UN site, http://www.un.org; the preamble to the *Universal Declaration of Human Rights* adopted and proclaimed by the United Nations General Assembly in Resolution 217 A (III)

instruments, therefore, go further than Canada's three-pronged policy by emphasizing what might be referred to as reaching out to others through discussion and dialogue. Indeed, how can cooperation and friendship be promoted without dialogue?

Yet we note that no measures to ensure dialogue with other ethnic groups were contemplated at the time the report was written, nor has this solution been adequately explored since then. In our opinion, the addition of this fourth aspect of "dialogue" is what can truly make it possible for all groups to accept diversity not only because they know and are prepared to tolerate the main characteristics of the other groups, but also because they want to understand and cooperate with others and gain their friendship so they can grow and be enriched by contact with them.

of December 10, 1948, in *Centre For Human Rights, A Compilation of International Instruments.* Volume I (second part), Universal Instruments. New York, NY and Geneva, Switzerland: United Nations, 1994, p. 1-7; and the preamble to the *Declaration on Cultural Diversity, supra.*

10.

Language of Work in the Federal Public Service: What Is the Situation Today?[1]

Matthieu LeBlanc

Introduction

In his most recent annual report (2012-2013),[2] Canada's Commissioner of Official Languages, Graham Fraser, asks whether federal public service employees feel comfortable working in the official language of their choice. The answer that follows is rather puzzling: "Even today, there are too many federal public service employees who cannot fully exercise their right to work in English or French in regions that are designated as bilingual for language-of-work purposes" (p. 29). It becomes clear from reading the report that it is particularly Francophones who have difficulty using their mother tongue at work, a finding rather reminiscent of some of the findings in the preliminary report of the Royal Commission on Bilingualism and Biculturalism published in 1965. In other words, despite the wishes expressed in the 1960s and the legislative provisions enacted over the years,

---

[1] Paper presented as part of the celebrations marking the 50th anniversary of the Royal Commission on Bilingualism and Biculturalism at Université de Moncton on June 14, 2013.

[2] Government of Canada. 2013. *2012-2013 Annual Report of the Office of the Commissioner of Official Languages*. Ottawa, ON: Office of the Commissioner of Official Languages.

the issue of language of work in the federal public service still remains problematic. What exactly is the situation today?

In this article, we intend to briefly outline how the language-of-work situation in the public service of Canada has developed since the work of the Royal Commission on Bilingualism and Biculturalism. First, we will consider some of the Commission's initial recommendations concerning language of work. We will then take a closer look at the development of the situation over the years, from the enactment of the *Official Languages Act* until now. In particular, we will point out the obstacles to using French in the federal public service. We will end by briefly presenting some of the major findings of a language-of-work study that we conducted in a department of the public service of Canada.

Royal Commission on Bilingualism and Biculturalism

The preliminary report of the Royal Commission on Bilingualism and Biculturalism was released in 1965. In the report, co-chairpersons André Laurendeau and Davidson Dunton referred to the many problems raised by the co-existence of the country's two founding peoples. One conclusion they reached was that Anglophones and Francophones knew little about each other and that, all things considered, nothing seemed to point to them becoming closer. The final report was published in six volumes between 1967 and 1970. Book III, which was released in 1969, was entitled *The Work World*[3] and dealt specifically with the work world as a whole; it made recommendations for the public service, stressing the principle of equality, and specifically socio-economic equality; it stated, among other things, that "[u]nless a language can flourish in the world of work, legal guarantees of its use by government services ... will not be able to ensure its long-term development" (p. 3). The authors pointed out the dissatisfaction of Francophone Canadians and what they perceived to be their inferior position

[3] Government of Canada. 1969. *The Work World, Report of the Royal Commission on Bilingualism and Biculturalism*, Book III. Ottawa, ON: Royal Commission on Bilingualism and Biculturalism.

vis-à-vis Anglophones in the work world. These findings were taken from research studies conducted for the Commission that revealed that Francophones were decidedly and consistently lower in average income levels, schooling levels, occupational scales and the ownership of industry.

With regard to the public service specifically, the Commissioners noted that, until 1966, no Canadian government had enunciated a general policy on bilingualism in the public service or on language of work. In their view, nearly all the linguistic traditions and characteristics of the public service put pressure on Francophone employees to become assimilated into an Anglophone environment. The Anglophone tradition of the public service thus seemed to be self-perpetuating. Numerous recommendations concerning language of work were therefore made. The main recommendations were as follows: that the federal government adopt the French-language unit as a basic organizational principle and that it provide for the creation and development, in all federal departments and agencies (including Crown corporations), of organizational units in which French would be the language of work (p. 265); that provisions be adopted concerning communication between the employer and employees (based on the employee's language) (p. 275-276); that positions be designated based on their language requirements (p. 277); and that drafting practices be changed by ceasing to do everything in English and then translating it into French, which meant that translation would stop being solely into French (p. 280).

Statutory provisions

Despite the report's recommendations, the *Official Languages Act*[4] of Canada enacted in 1969 contained no provisions on language of work in the federal public service. It was not until June 1973 that the government made a firmer commitment by passing the *Parliamentary Resolution on Official Languages*,[5] which marked the start of the introduction of the official languages program in federal institutions: establishment of language requirements

[4] *Official Languages Act*, R.S.C. 1970, c. 0-2.
[5] *Resolution on Official Languages in the Public Service of Canada*, June 1973.

for positions, expansion of the language training program, and the right of certain employees to remain unilingual (exclusion approval order). However, government employees were not given the right to work in the language of their choice until the new *Official Languages Act*[6] was enacted in 1988. The whole of Part V of the Act deals with language of work: "English and French are the languages of work in all federal institutions, and officers and employees of all federal institutions have the right to use either official language in accordance with this Part."[7] Certain regions of the country are designated as bilingual for language-of-work purposes.

The language of work situation from 1969 until now

Since 1969, and particularly since 1988, there has been progress on several fronts with the language of work: although the idea of French-language work units was abandoned after a few experiments in the 1970s, the government has nonetheless invested a great deal in language training for its employees and there has been progress with the representation of Francophones in the federal government and the linguistic designation of positions. However, as Keith Spicer, Canada's first Commissioner of Official Languages, stated at the start of his mandate, the task faced by the government with regard to language of work was very daunting. On the whole, progress has been slow. This is clear from the annual reports of the Commissioners of Official Languages since 1970. Here are a few examples: French as a language of work – one giant leap for bureaucracy, one small step for Francophones (1975, p. 15); language of work or language of the catacombs? (1978, p. 23); language of work: is there a choice? (1984, p. 69); the ship of state moves slowly (1987, p. 67); language of work – extended hibernation (1989, p. 111); language of work is the poor relation of the *Official Languages Act* (1992, p. 51); Language of Work: Is There Really a Choice? (1999-2000, p. 86); Where language of work is concerned, progress is slow (2001-2002, p. 68);

[6] *Official Languages Act*, R.S.C. 1985, c. 0-1, in force in 1988, S.C. 1988, c. 38.
[7] *Ibid.*, section 34.

minimalist approach towards ... language of work (2006-2007, p. 7); language of work: The situation is evolving, but too slowly (2008-2009, p. 20); increase commitment from managers to foster the creation of a work environment conducive to the use of both official languages (2011-2012, p. 69).

Studies on language of work

Based on the foregoing, it may be asked whether language of work is, in fact, as some have said, the "poor relation" of the *Official Languages Act*, since the application of Part V poses a great many problems and the obstacles to the use of both languages in regions designated as bilingual are often described as "systemic." A report on language of work in the federal public service published in 2003 by the Canadian Centre for Management Development (CCMD)[8] lists the obstacles most frequently cited over the years in publications of the Office of the Commissioner of Official Languages and the Treasury Board Secretariat, namely: the absence of work tools in the employee's chosen official language; the absence of central and personal services in both official languages; the absence of computer tools such as software in both official languages; lack of knowledge among employees of rights and obligations with respect to the official languages; the occasionally random designation of the linguistic profile of bilingual positions; the occasionally random designation of bilingual positions; information sessions that take place in one language only; meetings that take place in one language only; the unilingualism of supervisors and senior managers; the impossibility of writing documents in the first official language; the difficulty for many civil servants who receive language training to put into practice their newly acquired skills (lack of confidence, lack of opportunity, and so on); and lack of leadership displayed by senior management.[9]

---

[8] Matthieu LeBlanc and Patrick Boivert. 2003. *French to Follow? Revitalizing Official Languages in the Workplace.* Ottawa, ON: Canadian Centre for Management Development.

[9] *Ibid.*

In 2003, the Office of the Commissioner of Official Languages initiated a series of studies on language of work in departments and agencies in designated bilingual regions.[10] The objective was to identify systemic obstacles to the use of one of the official languages in certain regions. The three studies show the real asymmetry in the use of the two official languages in the federal government and, in particular, the predominance of English in many of the regions that are designated as bilingual for language-of-work purposes.

A case study: New Brunswick's Acadia

While it is true, judging from the above studies, that the systemic obstacles to the use of both languages in the public service are already quite well known, less attention has been devoted to the socio-linguistic factors that may explain language choices. This is precisely what prompted us to embark on a case study on the place of French as a language of work in the federal public service. Our study, conducted in a setting where Francophones are a minority, namely the Moncton area of New Brunswick, looks at language practices as observed at an office of a federal government department with the objective of better understanding language dynamics, language choices, obstacles and issues. The approach is entirely ethnographic (observation of language practices in various communication situations, semistructured interviews with participants, etc.). Very briefly, the following is what emerged.[11] First of all, the

[10] 1. Government of Canada. 2004. *Walking the Talk: Language of Work in the Federal Public Service*. Ottawa, ON: Office of the Commissioner of Official Languages; 2. Government of Canada. 2005. *Making it Real: Promoting Respectful Coexistence of the Two Official Languages at Work*. Ottawa, ON: Office of the Commissioner of Official Languages; 3. Government of Canada. 2006. *Towards Real Equality of Official Languages: Language of Work Within Federal Institutions of New Brunswick*. Ottawa, ON: Office of the Commissioner of Official Languages.

[11] See, *inter alia*: 1. Matthieu LeBlanc. 2008. *Pratiques langagières et bilinguisme dans la fonction publique fédérale : le cas d'un milieu de travail bilingue en Acadie du Nouveau-Brunswick*, Ph.D. thesis in language science, Department of French Studies, Université de Moncton, 496 pages (2 volumes); and 2. Matthieu LeBlanc. 2010. "Le français, langue minoritaire, en milieu de travail: des représentations linguistiques à l'insécurité linguistique," *Nouvelles perspectives en sciences sociales*, 6(1): 17-63.

study shows that the main benefit of the language policy for Francophones has been a considerable increase in the number of bilingual positions and, by extension, increased participation by them in the department, in part because of their bilingualism. Francophones have therefore been able to inhabit, so to speak, a professional space from which they had more or less been excluded for socio-historical reasons. Indeed, the significant Francophone presence has resulted in the normal and spontaneous use of French between Francophones, which is now standard, even if French does not fulfil all the same functions. While it is a language used *at* work, it is rarely the language *of* work.

On the other hand, our study confirms that, as in other public service offices, English is still the main language of work between Anglophones and Francophones (writing, meetings, training sessions, interaction with managers, etc.). The obstacles are often similar to those identified in the above-mentioned studies, but they also include the linguistic insecurity of Francophones, which is related to heavy contact with English and to the loss of French writing skills as a result of working in English for many years. In short, French is used very little by Francophones as a language of work. It must not be forgotten that, in this setting, in keeping with the "personality" principle, it is always up to individuals to exercise their rights and claim their right to work in French, in spite of all the problems this raises. What is also forgotten is that workplaces are governed by all kinds of power relationships, which are an important factor in language choices. But overall, the policy's main flaw lies in its implementation, since it is implemented *with no regard for the specific nature and needs* of the regions and linguistic communities involved. Because of its internal contradictions, the language policy also contributes to maintaining the domination of English as the language of work and, *ipso facto*, helps maintain certain inequalities between Anglophones and Francophones.

On balance, in light of the foregoing, we must conclude that what was envisioned by the authors of the Commission's report, namely a workplace respectful of both official languages, has been achieved only in part since the enactment of the *Official*

Languages Act. While the Act's implementation has been successful in some respects – language of service to the public and equitable participation of both linguistic communities, for example – it remains incomplete when it comes to the language of work.

11

A Look Back at Wage Disparities between Francophone and Anglophone Men in New Brunswick: What Has Happened Since 1971?[1]

Éric Forgues and Maurice Beaudin[2]

The Laurendeau-Dunton Commission was a major research undertaking concerning the place of Francophones and the status of French in the Canadian economy and society during the postwar period and the 1960s. Over the course of its mandate, the Commission received several reports on relevant issues. One of those reports, submitted by Raynauld, Marion and Béland in 1966,[3] continues to be cited today. It gave rise to a productive tradition of research into the connection between results achieved in the labour market,

---

[1] The results presented here are the results of analyses conducted by Nicolas Béland from the *Office québécois de la langue française.* We warmly thank him as well as the Office for letting us present them. Paper presented as part of the celebrations marking the 50th anniversary of the Royal Commission on Bilingualism and Biculturalism at the Université de Moncton on June 14, 2013.

[2] Éric Forgues and Maurice Beaudin are the authors to contact to ask questions or make comments: eric.forgues@umoncton.ca, mbeaudin@umoncton.ca

[3] André Raynauld, Gérard Marion and Richard Béland. 1966. *La répartition des revenus selon les groupes ethniques au Canada.* Ottawa, ON: Royal Commission on Bilingualism and Biculturalism, 4 volumes.

including wages and language. That research continues, although of course it remains marginal. But interesting books and articles are being published regularly[4] and the usefulness of the research is clear. Let me mention one of the major findings of the exhaustive analysis (four volumes!) done by Raynauld and his colleagues, which is clearly summarized in two lines in the first sentence of the report: [translation] "Geography is the main determinant of the operation of the Canadian labour market. Language is the second." As noted by Grin, Sfreddo and Vaillancourt,[5] this implies that many important economic questions are not independent of language and cannot be understood without considering language. Unfortunately, just as in 1966, this is still not done often enough.

However, it may be suggested, in 2014, that one of the findings made by Raynauld, Marion and Béland (1966) has become part of the Francophone collective memory. Census data from 1961 showed that, in Canada, Quebec and Montreal, Canadians of "French" origin were nearly at the bottom of the scale of average employment income by ethnic group. Only native individuals earned less in 1961. It is a little-known fact that Raynauld, Marion and Béland also dealt with the 1961 census data on New Brunswick for the Commission. Those unpublished data were looked at again by Vaillancourt and Roy in 1979.[6] In 1961, the "French" in New Brunswick earned 28 percent less than the "British." The difference was significant. But it was smaller than the corresponding 55 percent gap at the provincial level in Quebec. It was nearly as large as the 32 percent gap in Montreal, a city where, as in New Brunswick, there were large numbers of Francophones and Anglophones in 1961. However, the greater impact of the study stems from something else. Using techniques that were advanced for the time, Raynauld *et al.* showed that, in Montreal, nearly a third of the differences in income between the "French" and the "British" could be a product of discrimination against the "French" in the workplace.

---

[4] See, for example, Barry R. Chiswick and Paul W. Miller. 2007. *The Economics of Language: International Analysis.* Oxon, UK: Routledge, 596 pages.

[5] François Grin, Claudio Sfreddo and François Vaillancourt. 2010. *The Economics of the Multilingual Workplace.* Oxon, UK : Routledge, p. 17.

[6] F. Vaillancourt and R. Roy. 1979. "Les différences dans le niveau de revenu des francophones et anglophones au NouveauBrunswick," *Revue de l'Université de Moncton.* 12(1): 83-97.

What was the situation in New Brunswick from 1971 to 2006 in terms of the distribution of wages (the main source of income for the vast majority of people) by mother tongue (French or English) and bilingualism? Our objective is to trace this evolution using data from the public census microdata files from 1971, 1981, 1986, 1991, 1996, 2001 and 2006 while controlling for the impact on wages of individual differences in age, degree held, occupation, etc., in order to obtain net measures of wage differences by language.[7] We will also look at the link between wages, the use of French and English at work and the mother tongue of bilingual individuals in 2001 and 2006, the only years for which there are data on such use.

Wage Differences (in %) by Mother Tongue and Bilingualism for Men Aged 25 to 54 Fully Integrated into the Labour Market, New Brunswick, 1971-2006

%	1971	1981	1986*	1991	1996	2001	2006	2001***	2006***
Bilingual Francophones	-10	-6	-3	-5	-2*	-8	4*	-0.5*	12
Bilingual Anglophones	5*	-3*	0.7*	-1*	3*	3*	7	5*	9
Unilingual Francophones	-18	-8**	-13**	-13	-20	-13	-9*	-2*	3*
Unilingual Anglophones **Zero base**									
Main language of work: French								-12	-13
: English								--Zero base --	
n	295	776	875	1686	1659	1743	1732	1743	1732

*Non significant at a confidence level of 5%.

**Non significant. Few unilingual Francophones in the target population in 1981 and 1986.

***Controlled for language spoken at work.

Source of data: Statistics Canada, censuses, authors' calculations.

[7] The report to be published by the *Office québécois de la langue française* will set out the methodology in detail.

The target population consists of male degree-holders from 25 to 54 years of age who are fully integrated into the labour market in the most classic sense of the term. This population is the easiest to compare from 1971 to 2006.

In 1971, our estimates show a distribution of wages by mother tongue and bilingualism that is consistent with the historical picture. The same picture emerges from the subsequent data for 1981, 1986, 1991 and 2001. One exception during these 30 years: in 1996, there is equality between the average wages of (1) bilingual Francophones and (2) unilingual and (3) bilingual Anglophones. This exception may be due to the separate and prolonged effects of the 1991 crisis on the wage situation of Francophones and Anglophones. The initial estimates for 2001 go back to the historical picture for the distribution.

However, the same 2001 data, once controlled for the influence of the use of French or English as the main language of work, no longer leave any room for mother tongue or bilingualism as an explanation of wage differences in the target population. In 2001, working mainly in French or in English, is the only factor that determines these differences. In our opinion, this indicates that language of work is a reflection of the contours of the internal labour markets. Bilingual Francophones are under-represented by 25 percent in workplaces where the main language used is English, even with a significant Francophone presence in these settings. And the population includes virtually no bilingual Anglophones working mainly in French.

Is this division of the market by language mainly vertical, that is, between occupational groups in the same firm, or mainly horizontal, that is, between non-subordinate institutions? A comparison of wage data from 2001 and 2006 by language use at work could be useful for future research on the subject.

In 2001, where English is the language used most often at work, there is robust statistical equality between the wages of (1) bilingual Anglophones working solely in English,

(2) bilingual Anglophones working mostly in English and using French regularly at work, (3) bilingual Francophones working solely in English, and (4) bilingual Francophones working mostly in English and using French regularly at work. Between 2001 and 2006, this equality disappears. In 2006, the two groups of bilingual Francophones working mainly in English are in first place in the distribution of wages, tied with bilingual Anglophones working mainly in English and using French regularly at work. However, in 2006, and this is the major difference from the 2001 figures, the average wages of bilingual Anglophones working solely in English are well below those of the other three groups. This could well be a reflection of the documented increase in wage inequality in Canada over the past three decades.

Where French is the language used most often at work, there is robust statistical equality in 2001 between the wages of (1) bilingual Francophones working solely in French and (2) bilingual Francophones working mainly in French and using English regularly at work.

Therefore, according to our estimates for 2001, the net differences are equal between (1) the wages of the two groups of bilingual Francophones working mainly in French, and (2) the wages of the four groups of bilingual Francophones and Anglophones working mainly in English.

In the corresponding results for 2006, there is equality between the wages of bilingual Francophones working most often in French and using English regularly at work, and bilingual Anglophones working solely in English. We are talking about net differences here, as mentioned. Somewhere between 2001 and 2006, the wage situation of these two groups of bilingual individuals with different mother tongues, who did not work mainly in the same language, became non-differentiable. This convergence is noteworthy, since the wage position of bilingual Francophones working solely in French fell sharply when compared with that of bilingual Francophones using English regularly in addition to their main use of French, even though these two groups of bilingual Francophones earned the same wages in 2001 and worked primarily in French in 2001 and 2006.

Forty-five years after the work of the Laurendeau-Dunton Commission, our results show that the historical shape of the distribution of income by mother tongue and bilingualism disappeared in New Brunswick between 2001 and 2006. And they confirm that the situation of those who speak French at work remains an issue. It must be determined how the past and the present come together here. But as Raynauld *et al.* wrote, [translation] "[m]easuring and analyzing current inequalities based on membership is one process; identifying their root causes is another."[8]

---

[8] André Raynauld, Gérard Marion and Richard Béland. 1966. *La répartition des revenus selon les groupes ethniques au Canada*. Ottawa, ON: Royal Commission on Bilingualism and Biculturalism, Volume 3, p. 6.

Wage Differences (in %) among Bilingual Employees by Mother Tongue and Use of French and English at Work, New Brunswick, 2001, 2006

%	2001	2006
Employees working mainly in English		
Bilingual Anglophones working solely in English	*4***	*-10**
Bilingual Anglophones working mainly in English and using French regularly	*7***	*-2***
Bilingual Francophones working solely in English	*2***	*3***
Bilingual Francophones working mainly in English and using French regularly	**Zero base**	
Employees working mainly in French		
Bilingual Anglophones working solely in French	--------	
Bilingual Anglophones working mainly in French and using English regularly	--------	
Bilingual Francophones working mainly in French and using English regularly	-12	-11
Bilingual Francophones working solely in French	-11	-28
n	712	703

*   *Nonsignificant at a confidence level of 5%.*

** *At a level of 10%.*

--- Nonsignificant figures. Few bilingual Anglophones working mainly in French in the target population.

Source of data: Statistics Canada, censuses, authors' calculations.

12

A Look Back at Book V of the *Report of the Royal Commission on Bilingualism and Biculturalism:* What Progress Has Been Made in the Provision of Provincial and Municipal Services in the Federal Capital?[1]

Mark Power, Perri Ravon and Albert Nolette

B ook V of the *Report of the Royal Commission on Bilingualism and Biculturalism* ("Commission"), entitled *The Federal Capital*, was published in 1970 and contained 17 recommendations for the federal capital area.[2] In that volume, the Commission recommended that "the French and English languages have full equality of status" in the federal capital area and that the full range of services provided to the public by each level of government be available in both languages.[3]

---

[1] This text was written for the symposium entitled "The Commission on Bilingualism and Biculturalism Fifty Years Later" organized by the University of Ottawa's Faculty of Law, in conjunction with the Official Languages and Bilingualism Institute and the Centre for Continuing Education, in the context of the National Metropolis Conference held on March 13, 2013 in Ottawa.

[2] Government of Canada. 1970. *The Federal Capital*, Book V. Ottawa, ON: Commission on Bilingualism and Biculturalism.

[3] *Ibid.,* p. 41.

The 50th anniversary of the Commission's creation is an ideal opportunity to rethink the question of linguistic equality in the federal capital area. The following text focuses on the Commission's recommendations concerning the delivery of provincial and municipal services in the federal capital area and assesses the implementation of those recommendations.

In 1970, the Commissioners recommended that "all provincial services" and the "full range of municipal services" be provided in French and English in the federal capital area and that these linguistic provisions be "guaranteed by provincial statute."[4] It is interesting in itself that a Commission established by Parliament, whose terms of reference involved reporting upon the federal administration, expressly called for action by the provinces to guarantee services in French and English in the federal capital area.

However, such a choice is understandable. As noted by the Commission, while the federal government is involved in the development, improvement and cultural life of the capital through its agencies,[5] the Constitution appears at first glance to make no express grant of power to the federal government in relation to its seat of government.[6] Given the Commission's ambitious objective of creating a bilingual federal capital, it could not ignore the fact that the administration of the federal capital area, like all municipalities, is under provincial jurisdiction in Canada.[7]

---

[4] *Ibid.*, Recommendations 7 and 8, p. 63, 68.

[5] See, for example, the National Capital Commission (under section 10 of the *National Capital Act*, R.S.C. 1985, c. N-4, the Commission's objects and purposes are to "(*a*) prepare plans for and assist in the development, conservation and improvement of the National Capital Region in order that the nature and character of the seat of the Government of Canada may be in accordance with its national significance; and (*b*) organize, sponsor or promote such public activities and events in the National Capital Region as will enrich the cultural and social fabric of Canada, taking into account the federal character of Canada, the equality of status of the official languages of Canada and the heritage of the people of Canada").

[6] *Constitution Act, 1867* (U.K., 30 & 31 Vict., c. 3, s. 16, reproduced in R.S.C. 1985, App. II, No. 5 [*CA, 1867*] (s. 16 provides only that "[u]ntil the Queen otherwise directs, the Seat of Government of Canada shall be Ottawa").

[7] *Ibid.*, s. 92(8). On the question of the jurisdiction of municipalities, it should also be noted that, since the 1990s, the Supreme Court of Canada has repeatedly emphasized a broad and purposive approach to the interpretation of municipal powers (see, *inter alia, United Taxi Drivers' Fellowship of Southern Alberta v.*

The Commission described the concrete impact of the division of powers in the federal capital as follows:

> *We have gained the firm impression, after considering at some length the roles of the three levels of government in the capital, that the provincial and municipal levels—in combination— leave a far stronger and more direct imprint than the federal one on the pattern of life of the citizens.*[8]

While it is true that the Commission raised the possibility of joint action and cooperation among the various levels of government in relation to the capital, its finding that the provincial perspective "predominates" in the federal capital area made it opt for recommendations that required direct action by the provinces.

The recommendation that all provincial services be provided in both official languages in the federal capital area has been implemented with varying degrees of success. In Ontario, the *French Language Services Act*[9] was enacted 16 years after the publication of Book V of the report. Today, section 5 of the *FLSA* guarantees everyone the right to receive services in French from any office of a provincial government agency in a designated area, including all of the City of Ottawa.[10] In Quebec, on the other hand, no legislation has been passed to guarantee provincial services in both official languages in the federal

---

Calgary (City), [2004] 1 S.C.R. 485, at para. 6; see also *Shell Canada Products Ltd. v. Vancouver (City)*, [1994] 1 S.C.R. 231, p. 244-245; see also *Nanaimo (City) v. Rascal Trucking Ltd.*, [2000] 1 S.C.R. 342, para. 29; see also the Ontario Court of Appeal's decision in *Galganov v. Russell (Township)*, 2012 ONCA 409, paras. 23-29).

[8] The Federal Capital, *supra*, note 139, at p. 23. See also the Supreme Court of Canada's decision in *114957 Canada Ltée (Spraytech, Société d'arrosage) v. Hudson (Town)*, [2001] 2 S.C.R. 241, para. 3 ("matters of governance are often examined through the lens of the principle of subsidiarity. This is the proposition that law making and implementation are often best achieved at a level of government that is not only effective, but also closest to the citizens affected and thus most responsive to their needs, to local distinctiveness, and to population diversity").

[9] R.S.O. 1990, c. F.32 [*FLSA*] (before the 1990 revision of Ontario statutes, the Act was known as the *French Language Services Act, 1986*, S.O. 1986, c. 45. On the implementation of the rights set out in the *FLSA*, see Mark Power, Albert Nolette and François Larocque. Forthcoming, "La *Loi sur les services en français à 25 ans: constats et propositions*," *Revue du Nouvel-Ontario*.

[10] *Ibid.*, s. 5 (the City of Ottawa is an area designated in the Schedule to the *FLSA*).

capital area. The *Charter of the French language*[11] includes only a right to provincial services in French in Quebec.[12]

As for municipal services, while some progress has been made, especially on the Ontario side, it cannot be said that the Commission's recommendation that a provincial statute guarantee the full range of municipal services in both official languages in the capital area has been implemented.

On the Quebec side, the *Charter of the French language* provides only that municipalities of which more than half the residents have English as their mother tongue "may erect signs and posters in both French and another language, the French text predominating."[13] Not only does this provision not impose any obligation on municipalities, but it falls well short of dealing with the "full range" of services provided by municipalities to the public.

In Ontario, section 14 of the *French Language Services Act* provides that the City of Ottawa "may pass" a bylaw providing that all or specified municipal services must be made available in French and English.[14] It should also be noted that amendments

---

[11] R.S.Q. c. C-11 [*CFL*].

[12] See, for example, the *CFL, ibid.,* s. 2 ("[e]very person has a right to have the civil administration, the health services and social services, the public utility enterprises, the professional orders, the associations of employees and all enterprises doing business in Québec communicate with him in French"); see also the *CFL, ibid.,* s. 14 ("[t]he Government, the government departments, the other agencies of the civil administration and the services thereof shall be designated by their French names alone"); see also the *CFL, ibid.,* s. 15 ("[t]he civil administration shall draw up and publish its texts and documents in the official language").

[13] *Ibid., ss. 26, 29.1.*

[14] *Ibid., s. 14*

14. (1) The council of a municipality that is in an area designated in the Schedule may pass a bylaw providing that the administration of the municipality shall be conducted in both English and French and that all or specified municipal services to the public shall be made available in both languages.

14. *(1) Le conseil d'une municipalité située dans une région désignée à l'annexe peut adopter un règlement municipal prévoyant que l'administration de la municipalité se fera en français et en anglais et que les services municipaux au public, ou une partie précisée de ces services, seront fournis dans ces deux langues.*

(2) When a bylaw referred to in subsection (1) is in effect, a person has the right to communicate in English or French with any office of the municipality, and to receive available services to which the bylaw applies, in either language.

made to the *City of Ottawa Act, 1999* by the Legislative Assembly make it mandatory for the City of Ottawa to adopt a policy respecting "the use of the English and French languages in all or specified parts of the administration of the city and in the provision of all or specified municipal services by the city."[15] However, the Act specifies that the city is to determine the scope and content of the policy.[16]

Therefore, while it is true that Ontario has passed legislation concerning the delivery of municipal services in French in the federal capital, the scheme embodied in that legislation is essentially permissive. Section 14 of the *FLSA* permits Ottawa to adopt a policy on services in French, while the new s. 11.1 of the 1999 Act requires Ottawa to adopt such a policy but does not establish any minimum level or any criteria to be met in the delivery of such services.

A bilingualism policy has existed in Ottawa in one form or another since 1970.[17] The current bilingualism policy took effect on May 9, 2001.[18] According to its declaration of principle, the policy "recognizes both official languages as having the same rights, status and privileges." To this end, the policy includes objectives in five areas: language of work, language of service, cultural programs, complaints and communication.[19] The significant measures in the policy include R.1.12.1, in which the City of Ottawa commits to offering services in French whose quality and level are equal to those in English, and R.5.2, which states that all documents published by the city or its agencies and addressed to the

---

(2) *Lorsqu'un règlement municipal visé au paragraphe (1) est en vigueur, chacun a droit à l'emploi du français ou de l'anglais pour communiquer avec tout bureau de la municipalité et pour recevoir les services visés par le règlement municipal.*

[15] *City of Ottawa Act, 1999*, S.O. 1999, c. 14, Schedule E, s. 11.1.

[16] *Ibid.*

[17] *Canadians for Language Fairness v. Ottawa (City)* (2006), 146 C.R.R. (2d) 268, para. 16.

[18] On May 9, 2001, Ottawa City Council passed a Bilingualism bylaw (Bylaw 2001-170) and adopted a Bilingualism Policy (included in Bylaw 2001-173). The policy is available online. City of Ottawa, http://ottawa.ca/en/city-hall/your-city-government/policies-and-administrative-structure/bilingualism-policy [Bilingualism Policy].

[19] Bilingualism Policy, *ibid.*, Declaration of Principle.

public are to appear in both official languages.[20] It should also be noted that the policy does not merely state objectives but also includes mechanisms for meeting those objectives. For example, one part of the policy is devoted to language training for the city's employees,[21] while another part provides for the establishment of a translation and revision section.[22] The tangible impact of some of the measures in the policy is also clear. For example, the policy recommends that:

> *effective immediately, all external candidates considered for Level 1 to 3 management positions be bilingual. Any exceptions, after having undertaken a comprehensive recruitment effort, shall require Council approval.*[23]

However, while recognizing the policy's importance and the nobleness of its objective, we must note that it does not implement the Commission's recommendation. In the Commission's view, access to municipal services had to be *guaranteed by provincial statute* rather than merely being covered by a municipal policy. This can be explained in part by what the Commission perceived at the time as the lack of political will among elected municipal officials to provide services in French. In this regard, the Commission noted that a provincial statute should serve as an "external stimulus" to ensure access to services in French in the capital:

> *The problem, in our judgement, is not one of resources, but of attitudes. Until now, the provision of services in French has simply not been given sufficient emphasis in the scale of civic priorities. ... We consider that the balance of political forces in Ottawa municipal politics is by itself inadequate to bring about the necessary changes. Consequently some degree of external stimulus may well be needed.*[24]

The Ontario government has never taken such an approach. The provision of all or specified municipal services in French in the City of Ottawa is, therefore, subject to the discretion, will and demands of city councillors. It could be

---

[20] *Ibid*, R.1.12.1 and R.5.2.
[21] *Ibid.*, Part II.
[22] *Ibid.*, Part VII.
[23] *Ibid.*, R.6.3.1(i).
[24] *The Federal Capital, op.cit.*, p. 68.

reduced or eliminated by a majority of votes in City Council. As the Commission stated nearly 50 years ago, the provision of services in French and the status of French in the City of Ottawa are simply not given much emphasis in the scale of civic priorities.[25] The vulnerability of the City of Ottawa's Bilingualism Policy and the opposition to advancing the status of French in the City of Ottawa, therefore, justify the Commission's choice to recommend that municipal services in both official languages be guaranteed by provincial statute.

[25] See, for example, Philippe Orfali. 2011. "'Ottawa n'a pas besoin du bilinguisme officiel' – Jim Watson," *Le Droit*, March 25, online: LA PRESSE. CA, http://www.lapresse.ca/le-droit/dossiers/dix-ans-de-bilinguisme-a-ottawa/201103/25/01-4383165–ottawa-na-pas-besoin-du-bilinguisme-officiel-jim-watson.php; see also "Le maire d'Ottawa défend sa politique de bilinguisme," *RadioCanada* (September 21, 2012), online: RadioCanada. ca, http://www.radio-canada.ca/regions/ottawa/2012/09/21/004-ottawa-politique-bilinguisme-watson.shtml; see also François Pierre Dufault. 2013. "Une politique 'de bilinguisme pratique' suffit, croit le maire d'Ottawa," *Le Droit*, September 26, online: LA PRESSE.CA, http://www.lapresse.ca/le-droit/actualites/ville-dottawa/201209/26/01-4577601-une-politique-de-bilinguisme-pratique-suffit-croit-le-maire-dottawa.php; see also "François Boileau souhaite à nouveau la désignation bilingue de la Ville d'Ottawa," *RadioCanada* (June 5, 2013), online: RadioCanada.ca, http://www.radio-canada. ca/regions/ottawa/2013/06/05/010-rapport-boileau-ottawa.shtml; see also "Jim Watson dit 'non' à la désignation bilingue de la Ville d'Ottawa," *RadioCanada* (June 6, 2013), online: RadioCanada.ca, http://www.radio-canada. ca/regions/ottawa/2013/06/06/011-designation-bilingue-ottawa-watson. shtml; see also "Bilinguisme officiel à la Ville d'Ottawa: un parcours difficile," *RadioCanada* (June 21, 2013), online: RadioCanada.ca, http://www.radio-canada.ca/regions/ottawa/2013/06/21/010-caucus-francophone-juin.shtml; see also François Pierre Dufault. 2013. "Le bilinguisme officiel d'Ottawa absent du 'caucus' francophone," *Le Droit*, June 21, online. LA PRESSE.CA, http://www.lapresse.ca/le-droit/actualites/ville-dottawa/201306/21/01-4663722-le-bilinguisme-officiel-dottawa-absent-du-caucus-francophone.php.

13

The impact of the *Official Languages Act* and the role of the Commissioner of Official Languages in Canada

Extracts from an interview with Keith Spicer, first Commissioner of Official Languages (1970-1977)[1] by Graham Fraser, current Commissioner of Official Languages

Edited by Richard Clément

Graham Fraser: In your memoirs, you talk a bit about how you were at the university, how you left the university to work at *The Globe and Mail* but managed to keep a foot in the university environment, and through that, clearly developed – or maybe it's prior to that – relationships with some of the major figures of the Quiet Revolution in Quebec. How did those relationships develop?

Keith Spicer: Yes. The first way they developed was through the generosity of my colleagues, professors at the University of Ottawa who steered me to the bi-monthly opportunity to go on national television after the news and improvise a comment on the news, five minutes. So, what was it ... Jean-Luc Pépin, Guy

---

[1] This interview took place on June 17, 2013, in the offices of the Commissioner of Official Languages of Canada.

Dozois, Louis Sabourin.... They didn't have to do that but they knew I needed a bit of money; I was broke as usual and newly married, new baby, so they helped me to do that. As a result, I became, in a few months, extremely well known in Quebec. "What? An Anglo who can speak French like that and improvise like that?" I felt like, as I've said, the dog who plays the piano. He doesn't have to play brilliantly but the fact that he can do it at all astonishes people! So that was the first thing. I became very well known in French-speaking Canada.

The second reason was, I taught a course in French called *Le Canada français d'aujourd'hui* at Scarborough College at U of T [University of Toronto], and I asked Bill Davis, the Education Minister, to give me some money to bring in leading figures from the Quiet Revolution. I brought in 26 of them, everybody you could think of, beginning with Premier Lesage, René Lévesque, le Frère Untel for heaven's sake, and a whole range of them, Jean-Luc Pépin and Jean Pelletier. Anyway, the scenario I had was, I would bring them to my home the night before. The next morning, they would spend two hours with my class, being taped, giving a lecture and then answering questions. After that, I'd take them down to *The Globe* to have lunch – which meant horrible sandwiches – with *The Globe* editorial board. This was a win-win-win possibility. They wanted to reach out to English Canada, I wanted to get these guys in my class, and *The Globe* wanted access to these guys. So I was able to deliver to them pretty well all the top figures of Quebec at that time. That built friendships and acquaintances and really paid off later and, in many ways, led directly to my appointment when the Quebec press were talking about who they should name, and then *La Presse* came out with my name because I was the only Anglo they knew!

GF: The other preliminary task that you refer to is that you'd been asked, I think by Gérard Pelletier, to go across the country.

KS: I guess it would have been during the summer of '69. He had come to lunch at my place. He called me about a month later saying, "Would you like to be Assistant Undersecretary of State for Official Languages?" I'd say, "Thanks, I'm really honoured, but I don't think I'd make a very good bureaucrat. I'm too bohemian for that." He said, "Well maybe we need some bohemians, you know ..." The only thing I could think of was travelling – because I love newspapers – of travelling across the country, talking with newspaper editors. I got a flavour of the country – and the diversity of opinions – very, very clearly.

All the while I was at *The Globe*, I was making speeches in favour of the French, one way or another. I was invited to all the Francophone organizations to support their ideas, lobbying to get a French-language deputy minister of education in Ontario. I ended up being invited as sort of the agent of "the French conspiracy" at *The Globe*. They basically let me set the policy on anything French or bilingual and so on.

I always tried to keep bridges open, including to adversaries. In fact this is another story, but given that I had these contacts throughout Quebec, in the media, in the universities – I'd been invited to teach there, I'd given many lectures there, many speeches – I kept in touch regularly with the *Parti Québécois* when I was in your job. Not every week but once or twice a year.

I'd been in the job for about 18 months and I had come out with that teacup bridling statement that French should enjoy a healthy dominance ...

GF: A healthy dominance ...

KS: A healthy, *"une saine prédominance au Québec."* And my God that did not amuse the Liberal French, front bench or Trudeau. Some of the Liberal ministers accused me of sabotaging the Act. I said, "Yes, I've acted against the Act in order to save the Act in the long run, in order to assure a success because we cannot make this succeed unless we have Quebec society *dans son ensemble* on board."

GF: How did the government convey its pleasure?

KS: A phone call by Marc Lalonde – and he only called me a couple of times – he said, "Do you really have to say that because it doesn't help the cause. We don't stand for that and the Act doesn't say that." And I said, "If we don't have Quebec with us, this whole thing is a joke. We have to have Quebec with us and Quebec is not necessarily the Quebec that you want, Marc, you know. It's more diverse." That was at a time or another, an angle, when I was trying to establish the non-partisan status of the Office.

GF: When you say you studied with [Donald] Rowat,[2] you mean …

KS: No, no, I was a prof at Ottawa U and he was a prof at the other place, but he was writing books on the ombudsman and public information or access to information. We became friends. So my principal task was to start opening up the debate, transforming an angry argument into a civilized discussion with the people. And as regards to the Office, it was to radically change the image, to give us an image of a non-threatening, friendly, constructive place where you could go to be listened to and solve stuff. That's why I deliberately did not hire a full-time lawyer.

I spent 80 percent of our budget on public education. And we didn't have any lawyers … different Act!

Different Act! Different time! Above all, different challenge. Totally different. I had that feeling that if we didn't turn around, if we didn't create a new public opinion in both French and English Canada, and change the image of the Commissioner, it couldn't last.

I went to Trudeau with that one. I said, "Look, the Act says, even though I can do some things on my own initiative, it's just a throw away." It's clear that the legislator really wanted me just to receive complaints. I said, "If we only receive complaints, it will take a thousand years to make progress. I want to set up a preventive medicine service which will go to all the departments and the deputy ministers and say, 'Would you like us to come in,

[2] Donald (Don) Rowat (1921-2008), professor of political science at Carleton University in Ottawa, whose work contributed to the body of knowledge on the role of the independent ombudsman in Canadian Parliament.

and work with you to correct any problems, linguistic problems, by anticipation?'"

That's why, at that time, one had to win the battle of public education, of public imagery. As to the Act itself, I had to present it as a sensible, sane, overdue reform around this incredible inheritance we have of two world languages.

GF: How did you set up the Office? I mean, you said to somebody that your only administrative experience had been managing a two-hole outhouse.

KS: That's correct! I wanted to create, imprint the idea of an outsider that was almost all mini scandals. Even some of my most notorious *ad libs*, I had thought about it, to make a point, to tell people who we are, what we're doing. And I wanted to anchor the idea that I was not a traditional bureaucrat. I was not in the pocket of the government and, therefore, the two-hole outhouse.

I had spent a year as a speech writer for Guy Favreau, the Minister of Justice. So I had seen government from top, I had a good feel of what was going on, how departments worked. So when it came up, I knew that PSC existed. So when I walked into my office on April Fool's Day in 1970, it was empty. No secretary, nothing. Nobody to talk to.

The cupboard was bare. They had not really given ... because the stuff I wanted were the plans for implementation, but there wasn't any. I had to invent it all. Very quickly, I went around to see all the people that I needed to know. One of them, Gordon Osbaldeston, was in Corporate Privy Council. He wanted to immediately start cutting my budget. I said, "I'll make a deal with you: let me carry the can, I'll defend my own budget, you just keep out of it. If I screw up and I get hammered, then I'll take the rap." So he agreed.

There was the spirit of things. I eventually went to see the head of the Mounties. We joked, I'd say, "I'm gonna do an investigation of you guys, but ..." I joked, when it came to language, I said, "Let's have a kind of pact. I won't squeal on you if you won't arrest me." But you know, it wasn't serious, we were just joking; it was the atmosphere. They were all very nice to me because I was so much younger, 20 to 30 years younger than all my opposite numbers. They all tried to help in whatever way. They said: "Poor guy!" They all pitched in in their own way.

A figure behind me. I'd go to see Trudeau once a year. Maybe once more if I had something to show him. When we met, we'd talk about our kids first of all, because I was a single father 10 years before he was, so we talked about this stuff. But I would never take in problems. I would just tell him what I'm doing and then asked if he had any advice or comments. And one useful one he had was when I went with the complaints – I told you about the preventive medicine – I said, "I'd like to implement preventive medicine to get this thing rolling much faster." And he loved that idea. One other piece of advice he gave me, after my first annual report, I think he said, "Could you give me something like a report card so that I could see which departments are doing well and which are dragging their heels?"

GF: Oh really? I didn't know ...

KS: Yeah. Came from Trudeau, directly. I said, "Sure I will do that." So I decided to pursue it. I think the first one was on restaurants. The *Guide Michelin to Good and Bad Bilingual Restaurants*. This was not just frothy stuff, it was based on hundreds of hours of study of individual departments, in detail with a team of people.

I saw humour as a political weapon. Provocation and humour, together, surprise, and the idea was to pitch it, not to MPs, not to the government, but to the media. And it's because it was in the media, that the government would read it. I had to give the media some fun, some good copy. But it had to be solidly researched, so they can't knock it as frothy and frivolous. Once they dig into it, they'll see it's the real stuff. That was calculation. And I even had to use little pictures we had drawn. And then the other one was, I think, movies, hit parades, things like that.

Also, let's say, on the non-partisan front, I mentioned that I saw Trudeau once a year but I also saw the other three party leaders then. I guess it was Stanfield, David Lewis and Réal Caouette, of the voice from the past.

GF: What would you say were the most difficult terms that you faced?

KS: I would say the air traffic control.

GF: That would have been my guess.

KS: Yeah, yeah. I saw it coming a year in advance.

Here were the ingredients: you have the first generation of young trainee air traffic controllers in Quebec, because the Quebec education system until then had concentrated on forming priests and doctors and lawyers.

GF: Right.

KS: Now they're forming technical people and the feds are helping. And these guys are starting to want to advance. What did they see? A bunch of white-haired Anglos walking their way. This is explosive because then the *Parti Québécois* would jump on it. Eventually they created *Les Gens de l'Air.*[3]

GF: Right.

KS: It's a very, very political thing, really. You know how it ended. It ended with the *PQ* getting elected and the French controllers sent a bottle of champagne to the English controllers. Over that year, I established close relationships with everybody in play, in preparation for possibly playing a role: the English and French pilots, the controllers, the administrators, everybody.... One guy who didn't like me involved was Otto Lang, the [federal] Minister of Transport. "What are you doing

---

[3] Established in 1975, Association des Gens de l'Air is a not-for-profit organisation with the mandate to promote and protect the rights of Francophones working in the air traffic control industry. For more details, consult https://www.gensdelair.org/index.php.

meddling in our department?" I'd say, "Well, I'm trying to save you a big problem." It gradually escalated.

On the French side, you had a new union of Francophone controllers that didn't exist before. And they were determined, they were going to force French into the cockpits. There had been – I think it was in Yugoslavia – a case of double language ending up in a crash and I used this. We learned that there had been a fistfight in a Dorval control tower. And they'd say: "The English and French controllers, a couple of them, are setting up near-misses of planes to make the other guys look bad."

GF: Oh my God …

KS: I said: "Stop it this instant! I'll be there in two hours."

To the English controllers, I said, "You guys are from a different generation from these fellows and you're used to this but … one way or another, will you go in to at least listen to them to see if there is a way of doing this? As I said, I start with a principle and I don't care what the French-Canadians say about it. I put human life first, before bilingualism, before the *Official Languages Act*, obviously. And I want you to remember that, I'm on the side of the human life. "I will defend the French to the death in every other area. I will not risk your or my life." Thank God it worked.

When I got back, I called to gather the pilots and controllers again, and I held a big national conference with the media there, with everybody. I made sure that they agreed to test specific protocols in French. They all got up and I said, "Now, we're not leaving until we get some basic results here." And they did. They agreed to a long series of tests of trials, to see if there's a way.

Meanwhile, I guess the Olympics were coming up.[4] It was very, very tense. The English pilots were threatening to stop the Olympics by not flying to Montreal. I said, "You just have to come to terms or …" I used the Office, the neutrality of our office. I had already made absolutely crystal clear statements in favour of security.

---

[4] The Olympic Games of 1976 took place in Montreal.

I think about the week before the Olympics the government made a choice of basically coming down on the side of the English. They were afraid of a strike. They had to go for that. For the first and last time, I called Trudeau. He told me, "I've just come out of Cabinet" and earlier that day, Jean Marchand[5] had resigned.

GF: Right.

KS: I said, "I've been thinking all day about resigning and my analysis is, if I resign, *dans le sillon de* Jean Marchand, the language policy will be in ruins. The PQ will have a field day with that. They've got one of the Three Wise Men, Jean Marchand, and now they've got our friend Spicer – who now had lots of credibility in Quebec – both resigning. What's left, Mr. Trudeau, of your language policy?" And I said, "There has to be one English face on French television tonight. I'm willing to stay and do that, but I have to denounce you and your government very severely. This is just a heads-up on that." He said, "Thank you Keith, I really appreciate it. I think it's the right decision, I do appreciate the courtesy." That was the biggest drama of the whole time.

GF: Now, near the end of your mandate, following the *Gens de l'Air* crisis – and related to – was the election of *Parti Québécois*.

KS: Yes. Oh yes!

GF: How did that affect your position? How did you respond to it and what were the pressures? Were there new pressures on you?

KS: Remember that I knew all the leading separatists. I knew René Lévesque and Doctor Laurin Jacques-Yvan Morin. They were on a friendly basis with me. That didn't change anything. After they'd passed *Bill 101*, which wanted to implant

---

[5] Jean Marchand (1918-1982), journalist and Quebec politician. Marchand held several ministerial positions in the Trudeau government. In 1976, he resigned his seat in the House of Commons because he disagreed with a political decision that limited the use of French among the air traffic controllers in Quebec.

French as the language of work in Quebec, I called Laurin and said: "Bonjour Docteur! I just want to warn you. I'm going to make a press comment tomorrow and I'm going to say, one that I agree, as I said in my first report, that French should enjoy a healthy predominance in Quebec. My second comment will be that I don't think that your law is healthy. I'm going to attack you for that." The next day, the comment came out and I was on TV with it. He said, "I heard the comments of the Commissioner of Official Languages, and I know that he is in favour of the healthy prognosis of French in Quebec. We may have a difference as the way it's done, but we always appreciate his contribution." That was the spirit of the thing. It was not the kind of vicious attack you have normally, because these guys I had known for years!

Big advantage. Hum, what else ... Anything else? Did I mention, at the end of my term, what happened at the Quebec National Assembly or not?

GF: No.

KS: OK. I really blush to say this but I went for a farewell visit to this session of the Assembly and I had some business following up with the air traffic stuff. And Clément Richard, the Speaker, was a member of *Les Gens de l'Air*.

Richard pointed out my presence in the gallery and said: "We honour the presence of our friend Keith Spicer, everybody knows." And then the Liberal leader, Gérard D. Lévesque got up and presented a motion "To thank me for defending French language" and so on. I think Jacques-Yvan Morin got up and said: "Monsieur le Président, we'd like to *lever la séance pour cinq minutes*." They took a five-minute break. When they came back, he got up and said: "I, Morin, have met Mr. Keith Spicer several times and he's a perfectly charming, reasonable man whom we all respect. Obviously, we cannot vote in favour of this motion because it supports the idea of Canada which we do not accept." And then he said: "Mr. Spicer deserved a better cause to defend but, out of respect for the man" – I'm paraphrasing a bit here – "we will abstain on the vote so that the motion can pass."

GF: Oh my goodness! Wow.

KS: That's what happened. Checked it, *des débats*, March 31, '77. When I checked it that is the only time I had tears in my eyes over the whole caper.

GF: I bet.

KS: It was just everything I had dreamt of since age 15, at which time I knew somehow that French was going to become important in my life. And to have it in like that with a separatist Quebec National Assembly voting me thanks, a federal official, I mean that's not something I'm gonna say in the speech tonight, but it is in the book because it had to be recorded somewhere.[6] I wrote the book mainly for my kids so they will never forget.

How are we doing?

GF: I think, well … I think we're approaching lunch time. I think we've covered the waterfront.

KS: Yes. Did I say anything really indiscreet? …

---

[6] Keith Spicer. 2005. *Life Sentences: Memoirs of an Incorrigible Canadian*. Toronto, ON: McClelland and Stewart.

14

Bilingualism and Political Reality in Manitoba in 1983[1]

Andy Anstett

Background

In 1983, faced with a challenge to the constitutional validity of all Manitoban legislation since 1890, the government of Howard Pawley proposed an amendment to section 23 of the *Manitoba Act* to reaffirm French as an official language of Manitoba and avoid a massive translation burden. In exchange for reduced translation requirements an increase in French-language government services to the Franco-Manitoban community was offered. The amendment was characterized by the Pawley government as both a matter of principle in restoring long-lost rights and a cost-saving measure. Unfortunately, the cost issue initially took precedence in the ensuing debate, which was repugnant to those of us who focused on the principle, but as the debate progressed, the restoration of rights was more fulsomely acknowledged.

Manitoba had been a bilingual province since its creation in 1870, in the sense that legislation had to be adopted in both

---

[1] Paper presented at Université Saint-Boniface in the context of a symposium celebrating the 50th anniversary of the Royal Commission on Bilingualism and Biculturalism, April 16, 2013.

languages and each language could be used before the courts of the province; the history of how that duality of status was eroded is a sorry tale of denial by a series of governments over 90 years from 1890 to 1980, which included ignoring several Court decisions in the late 19th century that found the *Official Language Act* of 1890[2] unconstitutional as *ultra vires* the province. After the Forest[3] and Blaikie[4] decisions by the Supreme Court in 1979, the Sterling Lyon government introduced legislation in 1980 that attempted to avoid the requirement that all legislation be enacted simultaneously in both official languages, by providing for subsequent translation. The same Act repealed the *Official Language Act* of 1890 – finally recognizing Court decisions that had declared this Act invalid.

However, during this period Roger Bilodeau's challenge to the unilingually enacted *Highway Traffic Act*[5] was headed for the Supreme Court on appeal from the Manitoba Court of Appeal. The new government of Howard Pawley chose to attempt a negotiated solution rather than risk an adverse decision potentially affecting the validity of virtually all the laws of the province. The four parties to the negotiations were Roger Bilodeau, the province, the federal government and the *Société franco-manitobaine* (SFM). The official opposition (Progressive Conservatives) led by Sterling Lyon were aware of the negotiations, as a result of briefings by Attorney-General Roland Penner and had received a copy of the draft agreement, but were not directly involved.

In mid-May 1983, Prime Minster Trudeau prematurely revealed the proposed amendment to the *Manitoba Act*,[6] before the provincial government was able to make a planned announcement. The official opposition declared vociferous opposition to the proposed agreement and a firestorm of legislative and public opposition began. The official opposition Conservatives tapped into a broad antipathy to official

---

[2] *Act to Provide that the English Language shall be the Official Language of the Province of Manitoba*, 1890 (Man.), c. 14.
[3] *Forest v. A.G. Manitoba*, [1979] 1 S.C.R. 1032.
[4] *Blaikie v. A.G. Quebec* [1979] 1 S.C.R. 1011.
[5] *Highway Traffic Act*, R.S.M. 1970, chapter H60.
[6] *Manitoba Act (1870)*, R.S.C. 1985 App II.

bilingualism at the federal level. The government repeatedly attempted to explain the agreement without much success, recessed the House to hold lengthy province-wide public hearings – which I chaired – and then in January 1984, the government proposed changes to the constitutional amendment by placing the expanded French language services in statute law (*Bill 115*) rather than in the *Manitoba Act*. Also, during the recess, referenda were held in many municipalities, including Winnipeg, coincident with the late October municipal elections. The results showed a large majority of the public opposed to the agreement. This further emboldened the opponents and heightened their rhetoric. Shortly after the referenda, I was appointed Government House Leader and Minister Responsible for the French Language Services (FLS) constitutional amendment.

However, after the House reconvened in January 1984, the official opposition refused to appear in the House for required votes and instead allowed the division bells to ring for long periods. For the final vote before prorogation, the division bells rang for 12 days – 263 ½ hours. Speaker Walding's complicity with the Opposition by refusing to hold various votes, ultimately resulted in the government abandoning the constitutional amendment and corollary legislation on February 27, 1984. I have often wondered whether Pierre Trudeau's resignation two days later was influenced in any way by our failure to pass the constitutional amendment in the Manitoba Legislative Assembly and his disappointment with another step backwards for his vision of Canada (a vision that I shared and still share). In his speech to the House of Commons on October 6, 1983 on an all-party resolution supporting the *Manitoba Act* amendment, Prime Minister Trudeau described his participation in the debate as "perhaps the most important day of my life as a parliamentarian."

The political reality

The negative views of many Manitobans towards official bilingualism federally and in Manitoba were rooted in a very different perception of Canada that reflected the demographics of western Canada, which differ significantly from eastern

Canada. Their political reality was that their Canada was an English-speaking nation in which many ethnic minorities co-existed and spoke English. They considered French Canadians, at least those in western Canada, as simply another minority, and a smaller minority than other ethnic groups such as Germans or Ukrainians in Manitoba. They were not bigots; they simply had a different understanding of Canada. And, I think Manitoba's Francophone community recognized that different understanding. A button circulated by the SFM at the time stated: *"Nous ne sommes pas les ethnics."* I initially thought this slogan was very creative, but I soon realized that it spoke volumes about the political reality of the differing perceptions on both sides.

These perceptions were reinforced by ignorance of the linguistic duality of Canada since Confederation and the parallel duality of Manitoba from 1870 to the present time. That ignorance begot fear of changed status for other minorities. Otherwise rational people said they feared becoming relegated to third-class citizens of the province, because even if French achieved official language status, Franco-Manitobans would always have second-class status to the English majority. That ignorance speaks to the failure of our educational system, the mass media and other institutions to educate the public and the reluctance of governments to lead by shaping public opinion; that ignorance did not speak to bigotry on the part of many Manitobans who opposed the agreement. However, a substantial portion of the opponents were outright bigots who came out of the woodwork when their bigotry was legitimized by the official opposition and the referendum results.

The Beausejour area farmer who said his ability to farm would be compromised by making French an official language bespeaks of this ignorance; he thought he was going to have to learn to read French to be able to farm. He was concerned about labels on pesticide and herbicide containers. He felt personally threatened by changes he anticipated and feared based on the virulent propaganda of the opposition. That's not to say that there was no outright bigotry. Intense racial bigotry was demonstrated by some of the most vociferous opponents of the proposed agreement; there was a rabid radical fringe who were simply anti-French and hated Pierre Trudeau who they saw as the mastermind behind this ill-conceived agreement; and, they were not all right-wing Conservatives. There were also others who had their own political agendas, such as Russ Doern and Jim Walding, both of whom chaffed at being left out of the Pawley Cabinet. However, the official opposition Conservatives fomented that radical fringe to the point where the likes of grassroots Manitoba and others took over leadership of the opposition to the agreement; the Conservatives virtually became their captives. For example, the vitriol that was spouted at the hearing in Brandon revealed a palpable and deep-seated hatred for official bilingualism.

I recall telling my good friend, Harry Enns, who was my counterpart as official opposition House Leader that they were riding a tiger they had unleashed. He didn't disagree. Harry Enns always spoke frankly with me, but 'off the record,' of course. We had become friends when I was Deputy Clerk of the House in the 1970s. When Bud Sherman, as deputy leader of the official opposition, introduced an amendment to the constitutional resolution early in 1984, I immediately praised it publicly as going a long way towards reconciling our differences, but not quite far enough. Harry told me privately that my comments were not helpful, because they generated a lot of pressure on Tory caucus members from the public opponents to the amendment who now accused the Tories of caving in. He told me that the Tory caucus had had a difficult time agreeing to go as far as they had and this blow-back, that my comments had generated, was reinforcing the position of the right wing in their caucus, which included Sterling Lyon.

Pierre Trudeau was frustrated by our government's inability to get the Speaker to call the vote in the face of incessant bell ringing. He asked me whether we would consider replacing the Speaker and also offered procedural advice from the Table Officers of the House of Commons. I explained to the Prime Minister why we couldn't introduce additional motions since anything we introduced became 'ringable' and the opposition was so emboldened by the Speaker's refusal to call in the members that they would also delay votes on anything that might procedurally end-run their opposition to the constitutional amendment. The Speaker had effectively placed them in the driver's seat and by doing so protected himself as well – probably unknowingly.

Speaker Walding was personally opposed to the agreement. The Speaker was still a member of the government caucus, although appropriately, he usually only attended inter-sessional caucus retreats. Before the House reconvened in early January 1984, I briefed him privately on the changes we would introduce and his opposition was apparent from his questions and challenges. His subsequent procedural rulings were clearly influenced by his views. His rulings showed that he looked for any grounds upon which to deny the government progress in the House.

The decision to prorogue the Legislative Assembly was a purely pragmatic decision, with which I disagreed at the time and still think was wrong-headed. We could have waited out the official Opposition to see whether they would honour the two-week bell-ringing limit that the government had unfortunately agreed to the previous August; however, the majority of the government caucus didn't trust them. Of course, after prorogation, the Tories said that they would have kept their word, but Harry Enns made no such commitment to me; when I asked for assurances, his reply was always, "Just wait and see." If the Opposition rang the bells on the next motions that were required to complete passage of *Bill 115*, the government would have faced financial constraints because of an urgent need for supplementary funding as the March 31st year-end approached. With the House in session, this would have required a supplementary appropriation bill – which also would have been 'ringable.' After the House prorogued, the funding was granted by Lieutenant Governor's Special Warrants.

However, despite this funding issue and the political reality we faced if the government ran out of funds – the US congressional term 'fiscal cliff' hadn't been invented yet, a sizeable minority of the government caucus – 7 out of 29 – wanted to stay the course, because we strongly believed that the agreement was right in principle. This caucus minority was prepared to call the Opposition's bluff, so as to test their intentions to appear for the first vote and see whether they would also ring the bells for two weeks on subsequent votes. So the political reality of prorogation was pragmatism over principle, but it was also driven to a lesser extent by the sense that the constitutional amendment issue had forced the government off the economic agenda on which it had campaigned and been elected only two years earlier.

Profiles
of the Authors

Andy Anstett was, in the 1970s, Deputy Clerk of the Manitoba Legislative Assembly and became an acknowledged expert in parliamentary procedure. He was elected as MLA for Springfield in 1981 and served in the Howard Pawley Cabinet as Government House Leader and Minister of Municipal Affairs from 1983 to 1986. Anstett also served as the minister responsible for the French language services constitutional amendment in 1983-1984. Most observers cite his leadership role in the unpopular constitutional amendment as the reason for his electoral defeat in 1986.

Maurice Beaudin has been an economics and geography professor at the Shippagan Campus of Université de Moncton since 2003. Before that, he was a researcher and assistant director of the Canadian Institute for Research on Regional Development in Moncton. Beaudin earned an MA in Economics at Université de Moncton and a doctoral degree in geography at Université de Nantes (1997). Professor Beaudin has given numerous scientific lectures and published various works, in particular on regional labour market dynamics and skill requirements, Francophone minorities in Canada, and economic development in areas of the Maritimes. He has conducted research for organizations and for provincial and federal agencies. His current work deals with the rural exodus and new rural-urban configurations.

François Boileau is currently fulfilling his third mandate as French Language Services Commissioner of Ontario. His role is to receive complaints from the public and make recommendations on issues involving the application of the *French Language Services Act*. Before he became Commissioner in August 2007, he was legal counsel for the Office of the Commissioner of Official Languages, where he was in charge of landmark cases before the Supreme Court of Canada. He also played a key role in defending the language rights of Francophones by representing the *Fédération des communautés francophones et acadienne du Canada* (FCFA) before the Ontario Court of Appeal in the Montfort case. In 2011, François Boileau was awarded the Order of Merit of the *Association des juristes d'expression française de l'Ontario* (AJEFO).

Richard Clément is a psychology professor at the University of Ottawa. He is also the University Research Chair on Bilingualism and Society, and the founder and director of the Official Languages and Bilingualism Institute. His research interests include bilingualism, language acquisition, identity changes and acculturation. Clément is especially interested in the role of inter-group language communication in psychological adjustment and social harmony. He has received numerous national and international awards for his work and is currently a fellow of the Canadian Psychological Association and the American Psychological Association. In 2008, he was elected a fellow of the Academy of Social Sciences of the Royal Society of Canada.

Pierre Curzi spent the first 45 years of his career as a stage, movie and television actor. He was the president of the *Union des Artistes* for two 4-year terms starting in 1996 and co-president of Canada's Coalition for Cultural Diversity from its inception until 2005, when the Convention on the Protection and Promotion of the Diversity of Cultural Expressions was adopted by UNESCO. In 2007, he successfully ran for the *Parti Québécois* in the riding of Borduas. In 2011, after two elections and four years as an opposition member, he left the *Parti Québécois* and sat as an independent until the end of his mandate in September 2012. Since then, Curzi has continued working as an actor, radio commentator and engaged citizen as president of *Un Nouveau Mouvement pour le Québec* and the *Mouvement Démocratique pour une Constitution du Québec*.

Stéphane Dion was Minister of Intergovernmental Affairs and Minister responsible for Official Languages from 1996 to 2003, during which he crafted a renewal plan that was very well received in the community. He was also Minister of the Environment from 2004 to 2005 and Leader of the Official Opposition in the House of Commons from 2006 to 2008. Following the 2008 federal election, Dion retained his seat as member of Parliament for Saint-Laurent–Cartierville, where he has won seven times in a row since 1996. Dion is currently the Liberal critic for official languages, Canadian heritage and intergovernmental affairs.

Éric Forgues, a sociologist by training, has been the executive director of the Canadian Institute for Research on Linguistic Minorities (CIRLM) since 2012. Before that, he was the assistant director and a researcher at the CIRLM, from 2003 to 2012. His research focuses on the development of minority communities and the role of governance, social capital and community capacity in minority community development initiatives. Other research has focused on migration, income disparity and the model for addressing the health needs of minority communities.

Pierre Foucher earned an LL.B. from Université de Montréal in 1977 and an LL.M. in Administrative Law from Queen's University at Kingston in 1981. He has been a member of the *Barreau du Québec* since 1978. He has been teaching in the Faculty of Law at the University of Ottawa since 2008, in both the civil law and the common law sections. Before that Foucher was a professor in the law faculty at Université de Moncton from

1980 to 2008 and associate dean from 1987 to 1992. Specializing in language rights, minority rights and constitutional law, he is regularly invited to national and international conferences and has written extensively on these topics. He is currently a part-time analyst for the Language Rights Support Program and an associate researcher at the Official Languages and Bilingualism Institute.

Graham Fraser was appointed Commissioner of Official Languages in October 2006 for a seven-year term. In October 2013, he was reappointed for another three years. Since his appointment, Fraser has been involved in many important issues concerning the language rights of Canadians. Under him, the Office of the Commissioner of Official Languages has handled such high-profile language issues as the Vancouver 2010 Olympic and Paralympic Winter Games, the 40th anniversary of the *Official Languages Act*, including the "Déjà Vu: 40 Years of Language and Laughter in Political Cartoons" exhibition, and the creation of the Award of Excellence – Promotion of Linguistic Duality, given to an individual or an organization in Canada in recognition of outstanding contributions to the promotion of linguistic duality in Canada or abroad, or the development of official language communities.

Raymond-M. Hébert is an emeritus professor of political science and Canadian studies at Université de Saint-Boniface. He has published numerous articles on language minorities in Canada and associated constitutional issues. In 2005, he was awarded the Alexander Kennedy Isbister Award for best non-fiction work by a Manitoban in 2004 for his book *Manitoba's French-Language Crisis: A Cautionary Tale*. Hébert is also well known in Canada as a political analyst for the media, in both French and English, in particular with respect to language issues. He is a past president (1998-2000) of the Association for Canadian Studies. In 2013, he coordinated the very first language rights course offered by the Faculty of Law at the University of Manitoba. Before his teaching career, which lasted from

1980 until his retirement in 2009, Hébert was Manitoba's first Assistant Deputy Minister of the *Bureau de l'éducation française* (1976-1979).

Michelle Landry is a sociology professor at the Shippagan Campus of Université de Moncton. She holds a Ph.D. in Sociology from Université Laval, and her research focuses on issues related to the power and socio-political structure of language minorities, in particular Acadians in New Brunswick. Landry is also interested in nationalism, collective representations and the identities of Francophone communities in Canada. Her approach is primarily socio-historical and socio-political.

Matthieu LeBlanc is an associate professor of translation in Université de Moncton's translation and languages department. He teaches introductory, general and specialized translation; comparative stylistics; writing and editing. His research focuses on translation science (status of translators, role of translation in a minority setting, tools), socio-linguistics and language planning. LeBlanc wrote his Ph.D. thesis, which he defended in 2008, on the language practices of a department of the federal public service in a Francophone minority setting. He found that, despite the progress made on official languages over the last 40 years, language of work remains the poor cousin of Canada's *Official Languages Act*, at least in Francophone minority settings.

Albert Nolette works as a lawyer with Field LLP in Edmonton. He focuses his practice on litigation, labour law, employment law and language rights. He is a member of the board of directors of the *Association canadienne-française de l'Alberta* (ACFA).

Mark Power is a partner at Power Law, a firm he founded in 2014. Power focuses his practice on litigation and constitutional law, and has considerable expertise in education law and language rights. He has been solicitor of record in more than 25 cases before the Supreme Court of Canada and has provided advice in other cases before that court. Power has published extensively in peer-reviewed journals in the field of language rights, and he is the author of the chapter on education in the reference work *Language Rights in Canada*, 3rd ed., edited by the Honourable Michel Bastarache, C.C., Q.C., and Michel Doucet. He began his law career after clerking for the Honourable Mr. Justice Michel Bastarache, C.C., Q.C., at the Supreme Court of Canada.

Perri Ravon works as a lawyer at Power Law in Ottawa. In 2011-2012, Ravon clerked for the Honourable Madam Justice Marie Deschamps at the Supreme Court of Canada. She focuses her practice on litigation and constitutional law, and has worked on numerous language rights cases. She co-authored the chapters on language rights in international law and the right to receive public services in either official language in the reference work *Language Rights in Canada*, 3rd ed., edited by the Honourable Michel Bastarache, C.C., Q.C., and Michel Doucet.

Ingride Roy earned an LL.L. from the University of Ottawa in 1992 and became a member of the *Barreau du Québec* in 1993. She began her career in the fields of administrative law and municipal law, and was a municipal court prosecutor in Saint-Raymond from 1993 to 1996. She then worked as a legal advisor for federal ministers and the Commissioner of Official Languages in various cases dealing with constitutional law and language rights, in particular the *Beaulac* case before the Supreme Court of Canada. She also helped conduct a number of Canada-wide studies on language rights. In 1998, Roy completed a *Diplôme d'études approfondies* (D.E.A.) in international law at Université d'Aix-Marseille III and, in 2005, a Ph.D. in International Law at the University of Ottawa. Since then, she has been an instructor at Université de Sherbrooke and Université de Montréal, teaching public international law and constitutional law, while pursuing her career as a lawyer.

Sherry Simon is a professor in the Département d'études françaises at Concordia University. Her areas of research include Quebec literature and culture, translation studies and multilingual cities, and she has published extensively in these areas. Among her recent publications are *Translating Montreal* (2006), translated into French by Pierrot Lambert as *Traverser Montréal* (2008), and *Cities in Translation: Intersections of Language and Memory* (2012), translated into French by Pierrot Lambert as *Villes en traduction: Trieste, Calcutta, Barcelone et Montréal* (2013). She is a member of the Royal Society of Canada and the *Académie des lettres du Québec*; she was a Killam Research Fellow from 2009 to 2011.

Keith Spicer was the first Commissioner of Official Languages, appointed in 1970 for a seven-year term. At that time, he stated that he would seek to "uncover all infractions of the Act and prevent their repetition." He was delighted with a resolution by Parliament in 1973 to make English and French the languages of work in the federal government.

Roger Turenne holds an M.A. in Political Science from the University of Manitoba (1970). A research officer for the Royal Commission on Bilingualism and Biculturalism in 1965, he contributed to the study by Murray S. Donnelly on the participation of minority groups in the municipal institutions of the metropolitan area of Winnipeg. As a Canadian diplomat, he was posted to Paris with the Permanent Delegation of Canada to the United Nations Educational, Scientific and Cultural Organization, and to Canadian embassies in Kinshasa and Stockholm. As a special advisor to the Premier of Manitoba on French-language services, Turenne was the architect of language policies announced by Premier Pawley in 1982 and by Premier Filmon in 1989. He was also a consultant for the Government of Yukon to develop a language policy for the territory. He is the author of *Mon pays noir sur blanc – Regards sur le Manitoba français* (Les Éditions du Blé, Saint-Boniface, 1981).

Other titles published by INVENIRE

Titles in the Collaborative Decentred Metagovernance Series